Table of Contents

AF440937

BVCC

Word Processing for Seniors

by Len Nasman, PhD

- ➢ **Large Print**
- ➢ **Step-by-Step Projects**
- ➢ **Insert Graphic Images**
- ➢ **Insert Tables & Frames**
- ➢ **Create Books**
- ➢ **Create Newsletters**
- ➢ **Create Greeting Cards**

for Windows, Linux, Mac

About the Author

Len Nasman has a varied background in engineering graphics and education. He started his career as a drafter at Bell Labs in Whippany, NJ and, after completing his bachelor's degree, worked for a number of years as a Design Engineer in the aerospace industry. He taught Drafting and Design at Trinidad State Community College in Colorado, and received his Master's and Ph. D. degrees in Vocational Technical Education from Colorado State University. After nine years in Vocational Technical Teacher Education in Colorado and Texas, he returned to his roots by accepting an assignment in the Engineering Graphics Department at The Ohio State University in 1982. 

After 17 years at Ohio State, Len moved full time to Microcomputer Education Systems Inc. (the company he founded) to develop CAD (Computer Aided Design) books, video tapes, and other instructional materials. Over 100,000 copies of his books and instructional videotapes have been distributed world-wide. (A recent search on World Cat revealed that libraries as far away as Hong Kong, South Africa, and Singapore have copies of Len's Engineering Drawing Videos.)

Len is now retired and is busier then ever with his hobbies which include: music, photography, table tennis, and playing with computers. Since moving to Bristol Village Ohio, Len has been active in the local Computer Club and has been working with the Sight and Sound Committee maintaining and upgrading audio/video equipment and 'working the booth' for local programs that are transmitted to Bristol Village on cable television. He developed the Bristol Village residents web site (www.bvres.org) and in the Computer Club section of the site has place a number of links to tutorials including instructions for using LibreOffice.

The first thing to do is to make sure the illustrations on your computer display are similar to the ones in this book. Here's how.

NOTE: The illustrations in this book are from *LibreOffice version 7*. If this program in not installed on your computer, see *Appendix A*.

✔ Start *LibreOffice* and start a new **Writer Document**.

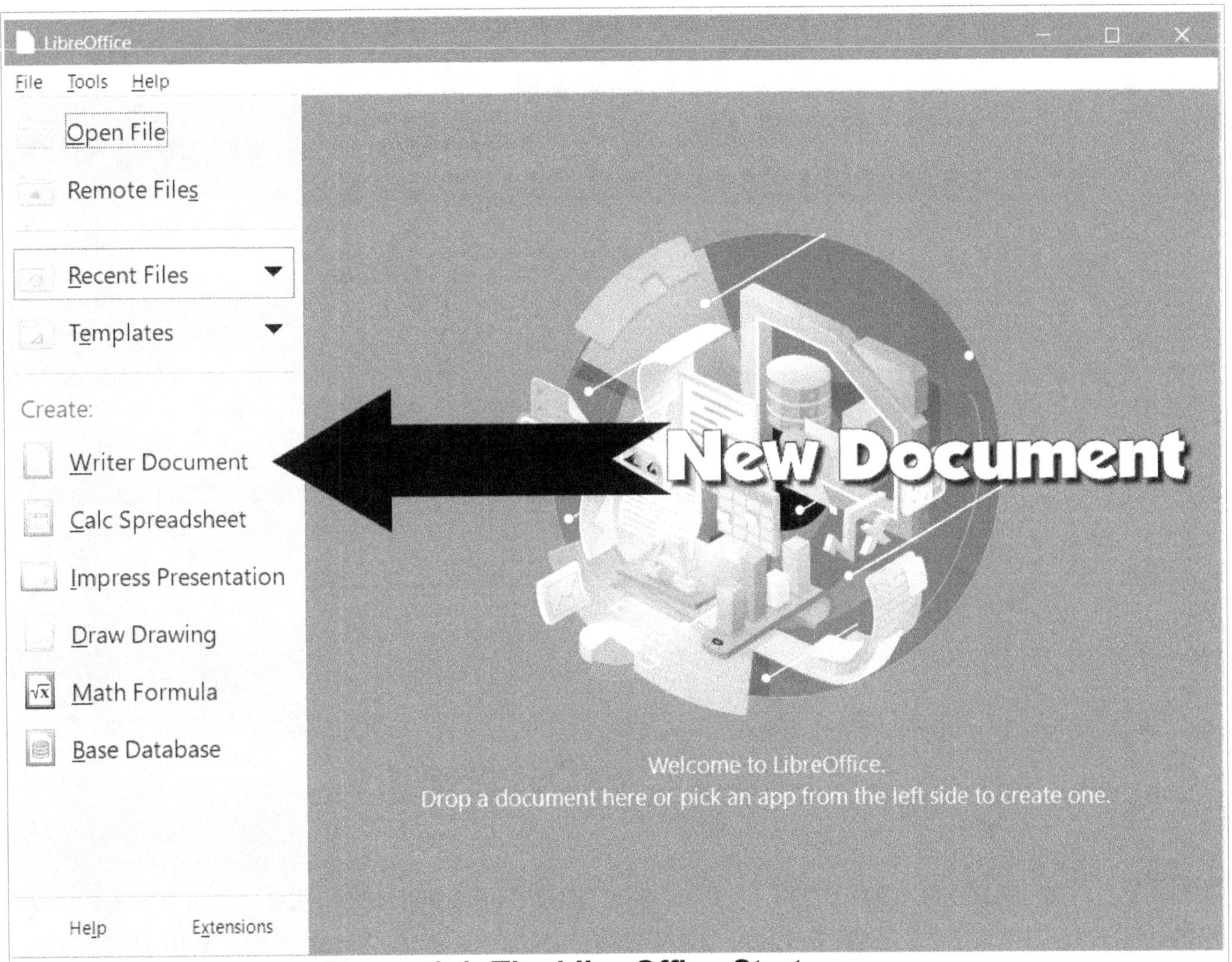

Figure 1-1, The LibreOffice Start screen.

You should now have a new document on your display. The *Titlebar* will show the *Document Name* and the name of the current program in the display window.

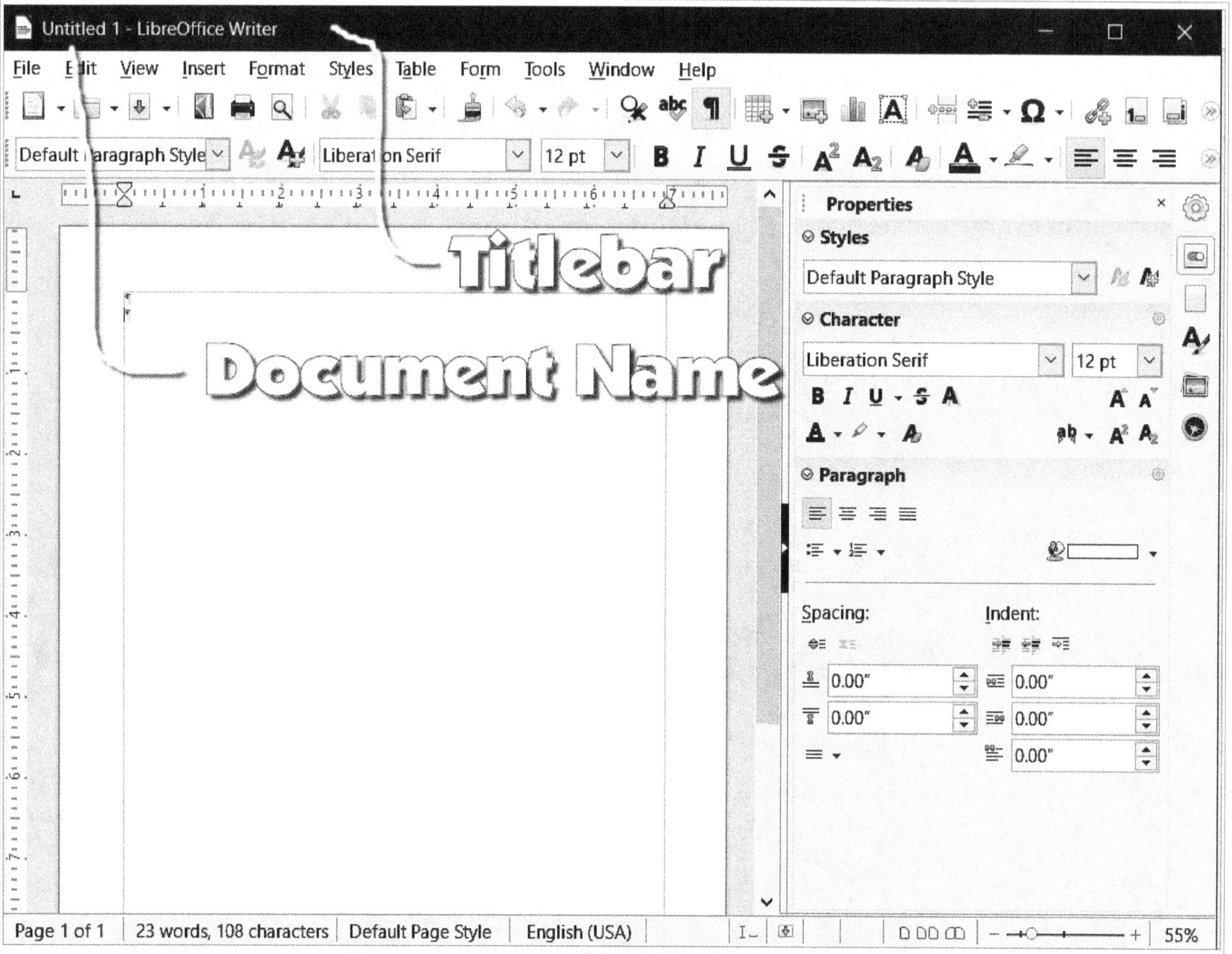

Figure 1-2, New *Untitled* document.

NOTE: The screen captures in this document have been set to a lower resolution to make them easier to read. Your screen resolution will probably be different.

Next, you should check the user interface to make sure it agrees with the illustrations in this book.

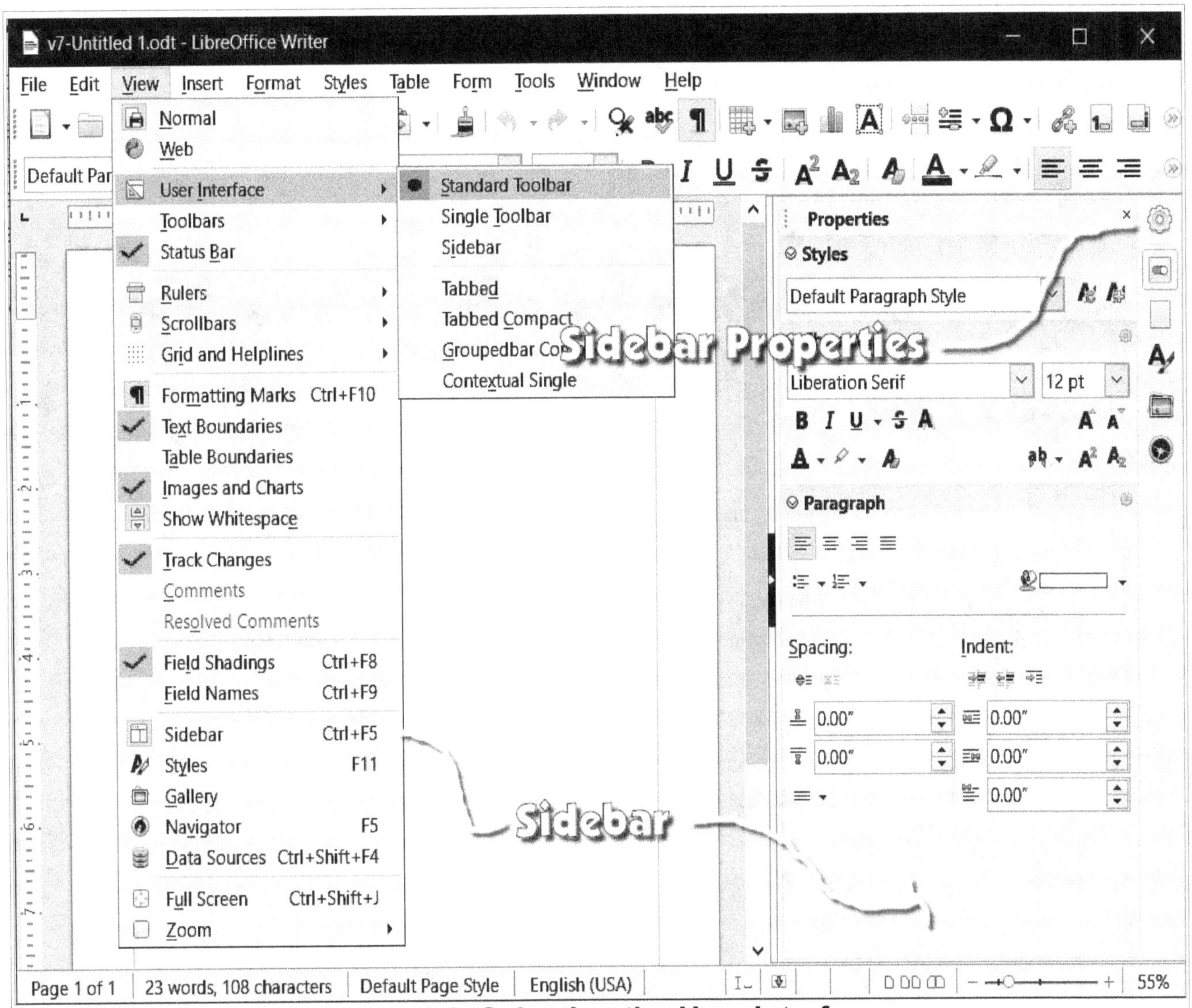

Figure 1-3, Selecting the User Interface.

✔ From the *Menubar*, select **View, User interface, Standard Toolbar.**

✔ If the *Sidebar* is not on, select it from the drop down *View* menu.

✔ If the *Sidebar* does not show the *Properties* options, select the **Sidebar Options tool** in the upper right corner of the display, and then select **Properties**.

LibreOffice provides a number of different icon styles for the tool-bar. In this set of projects, the *Elementary* Icon style was used. Here is how to change the *Icon style.*

✓ From the *Menubar*, select **Tools, Options, View**. Then select the desired Ion style and size. (See Figure 1-4.)

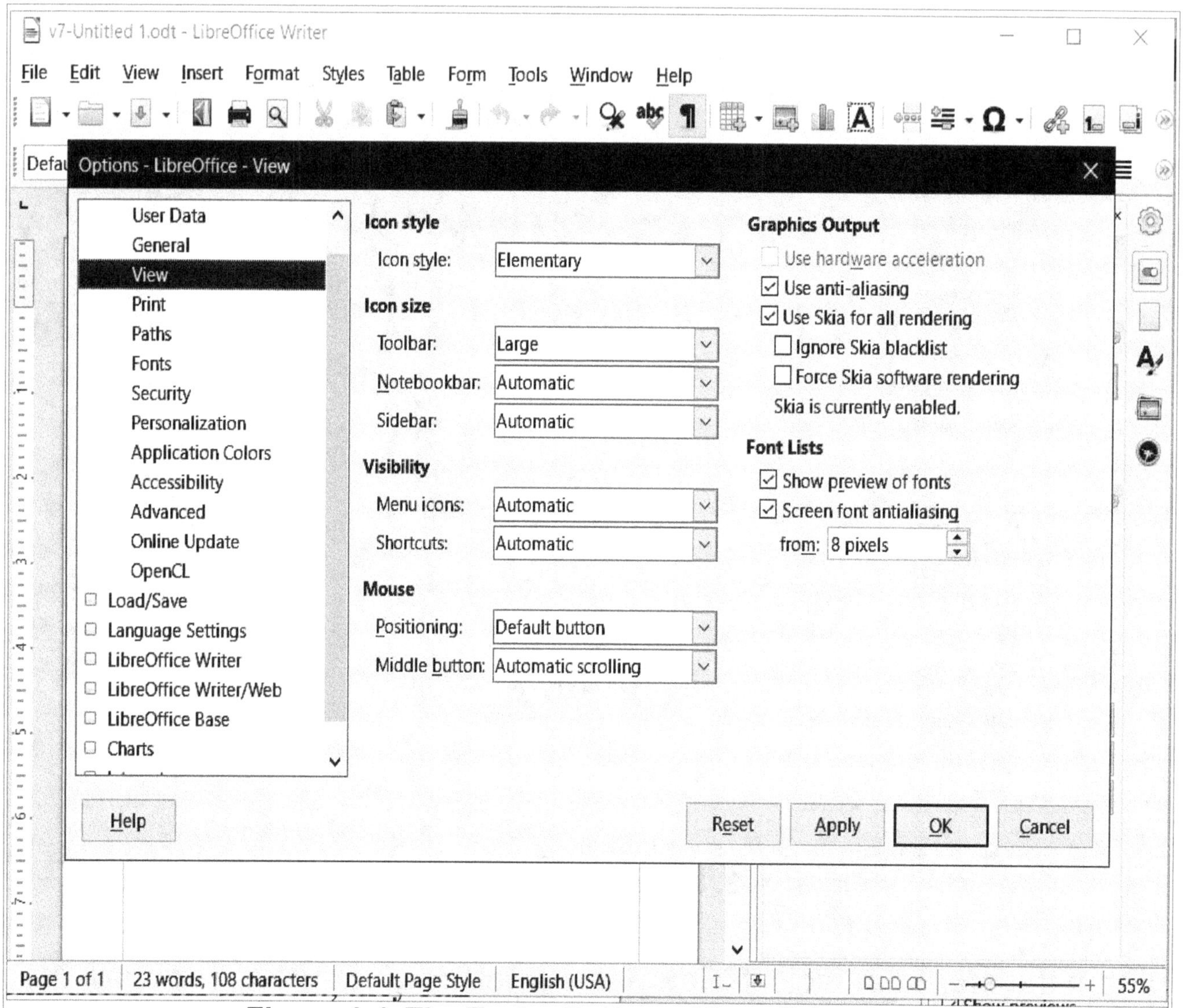

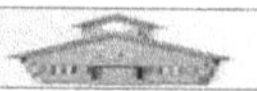

Figure 1-4, The Tools, Options, View dialog box.

There is another tool to turn on in the user interface. This is the *Formatting Marks tool.* This tool is very important because it shows the non printing characters that control text formatting. The non printing characters include *paragraph, tab* and *space* characters. Some typists, who are used to formatting as they type, don't like the looks of the non formatting characters. As a result, they can become frustrated when the stupid printer spits out blank pages, or when alignments change with different font selections. If you want to be a serious word processor instead of a frustrated typist, keep the *Formatting Marks* tool toggled **ON**.

✔ If the *Paragraph* character is not on the display, from the *Toolbar* select the **Formatting Marks tool toggle**.

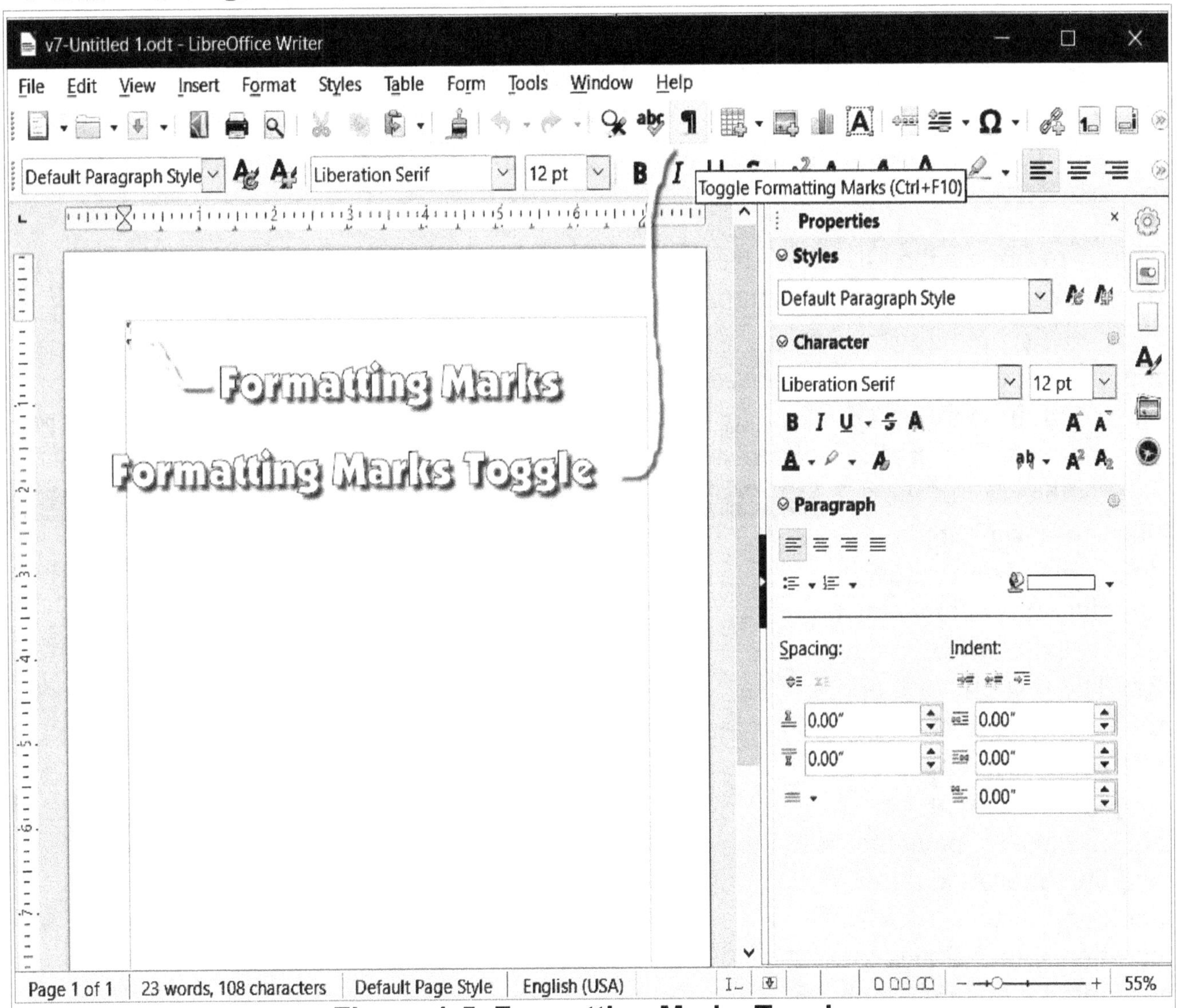

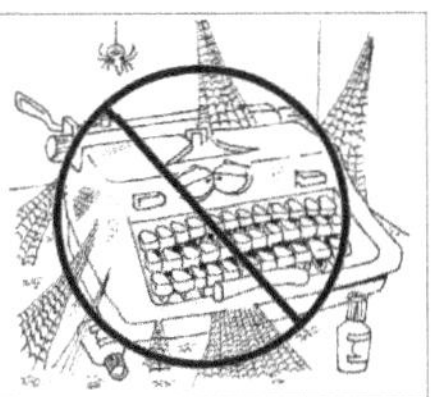

Figure 1-5, Formatting Marks Toggle.

OK, now it's time to start entering text. Remember, this is not like typing on an old typewriter. One big difference from typing is you only use a carriage return (or

the Enter Key) when you come to the end of a *paragraph.* The Word Processing system automatically wraps the words when it runs out of space at the end of a line. When you press the *Enter Key,* a new paragraph will be started. A little later, you will see how to change the font used in paragraphs. For now, just enter a few sentences.

✔ Place the text cursor on the first line of your document and type some text. If you are at a loss for words, use the ones below. Enter at least three paragraphs of text. Do not add empty paragraphs between paragraphs.

Observe that your text will not have spacing between lines. You will see how to change this after you have entered your three paragraphs.

This is my first LibreOffice Writer document. I am now typing a new paragraph into the document. I will not press the enter key until I am finished with the first paragraph.

I am now typing a second paragraph. It is important to remember that in word processing, paragraphs are ended by pressing the enter key. It is also important to know that a paragraph in word processing may consist of several sentences, one sentence, one word, or even no words at all. I will press the enter key to end this paragraph.

This is the start of the third paragraph in the document. The vertical line that moves along as I type is called the text cursor. The text cursor marks the point where new characters will appear as I type. There are a number of ways to move the text cursor around the document. I will learn a number of techniques for moving the text cursor as I go through these tutorials.

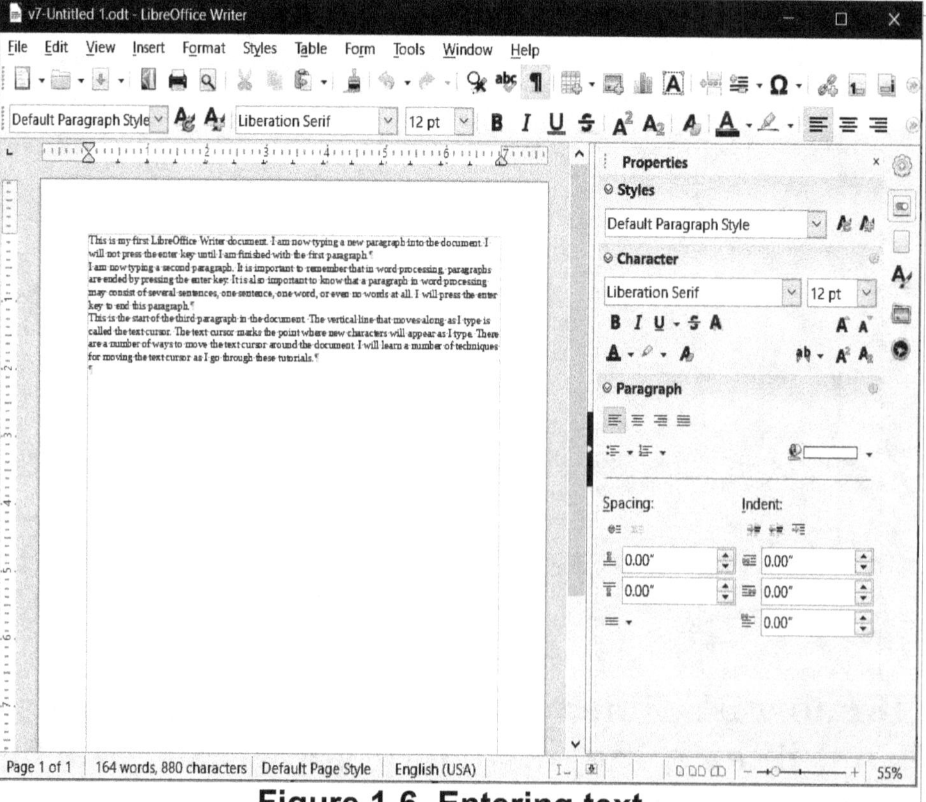

Figure 1-6, Entering text.

If you have entered text on a computer before, you proba-

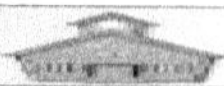

bly know that you can use different font styles. In this lesson, you will go one step farther and learn about *Paragraph Styles*.

Before we change the *Paragraph Style* of the text, we need to take a side trip to learn a selection trick.

✔ From the *Menubar*, select **Edit**, **Select All**.

NOTE: Observe that the pop down menu shows that the short-cut to *Select All* is **Ctrl+A**. This means hold the **Ctrl** Key down and press the **A** key. The is a good trick to remember. It will save you some time in the long run.

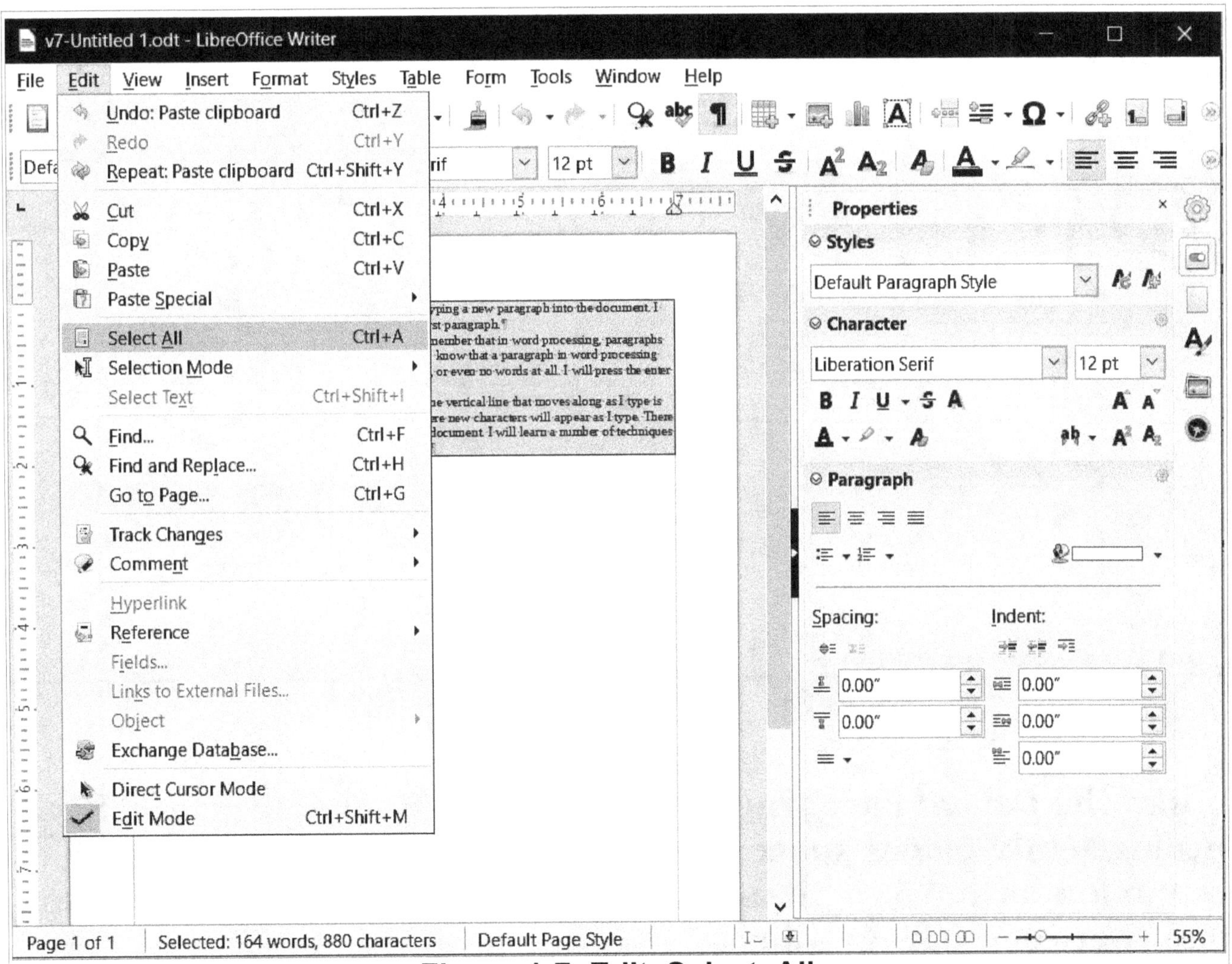

Figure 1-7, Edit, Select, All.

Now that all of the text is selected, the paragraph style for all selected paragraphs will be changed at the same time.

Selecting a Paragraph Style

✓ From the **Toolbar** (see Figure 1-8) select the **Text Body** *Paragraph Style*.

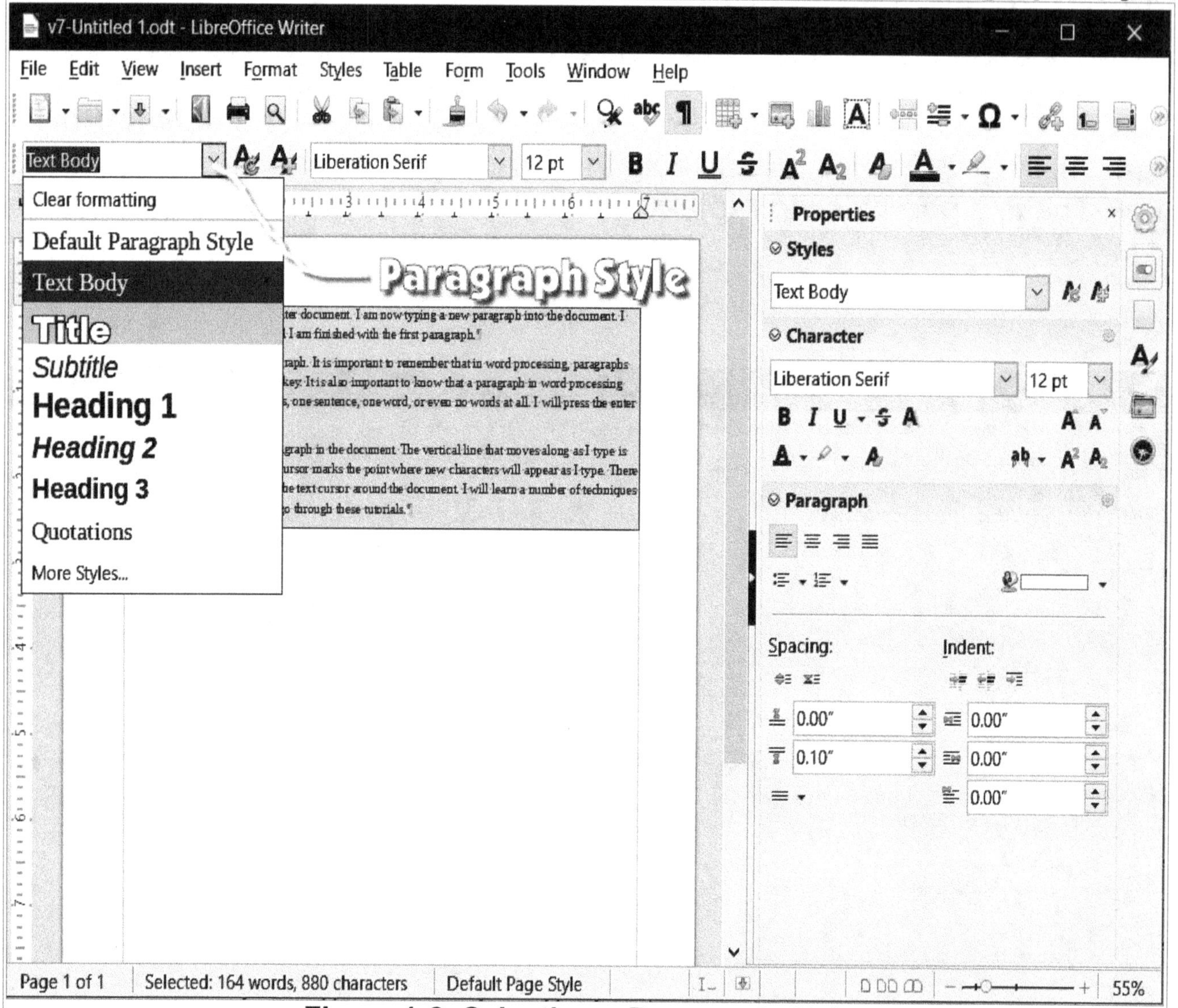

Figure 1-8, Selecting a Paragraph Style.

Unlike the *Default* Paragraph Style, the *Text Body* Paragraph Style automatically places space between paragraphs. This means that you no longer have to hit an extra *Enter Key* every time you want space between paragraphs.

But it gets even better. In addition to spacing between paragraphs, *Paragraph Styles* include a large collection of settings for paragraphs. You will learn how to use these settings in a future lesson.

For now, let's add a title paragraph. But first, a couple more tricks to add that will help you become a power user.

✓ Move the mouse pointer anywhere in the document and press the *left* mouse button **once.**

You should see a flashing text cursor where you positioned the mouse pointer.

✓ You can precisely control the position of the text cursor by pressing the *arrow keys* on you keyboard... try it. Use the arrow keys to move the text cursor around the document.

Here are some important short-cuts to remember.

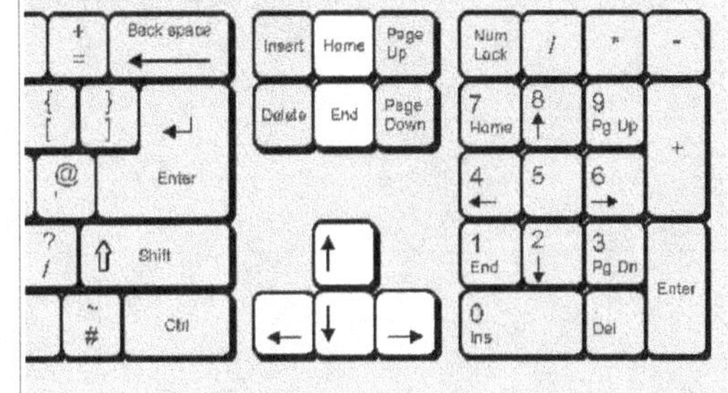

✓ Press the **Home Key** and see the text cursor jump to the beginning of the current line.

✓ Press the **End Key** and see the text cursor jump to the end of the current line.

✓ Hold the **Crtl Key** down and press the **End Key** [Ctrl+End] and see the text cursor jump to the end of the document.

✓ Hold the **Ctrl Key** down and press the **Home Key** [Ctrl+Home] and see the text cursor jump to the beginning of the document.

Now, let's add a title paragraph to our document.

✓ With the *text cursor* at the *top left* corner of the text, press the **Enter Key** to add a new paragraph.

✓ With the text cursor in the new paragraph, enter My First Document.

✓ With the text cursor in the *My First Document* paragraph, select the **Title Paragraph Style**.

Your document should now look similar to Figure 1-9.

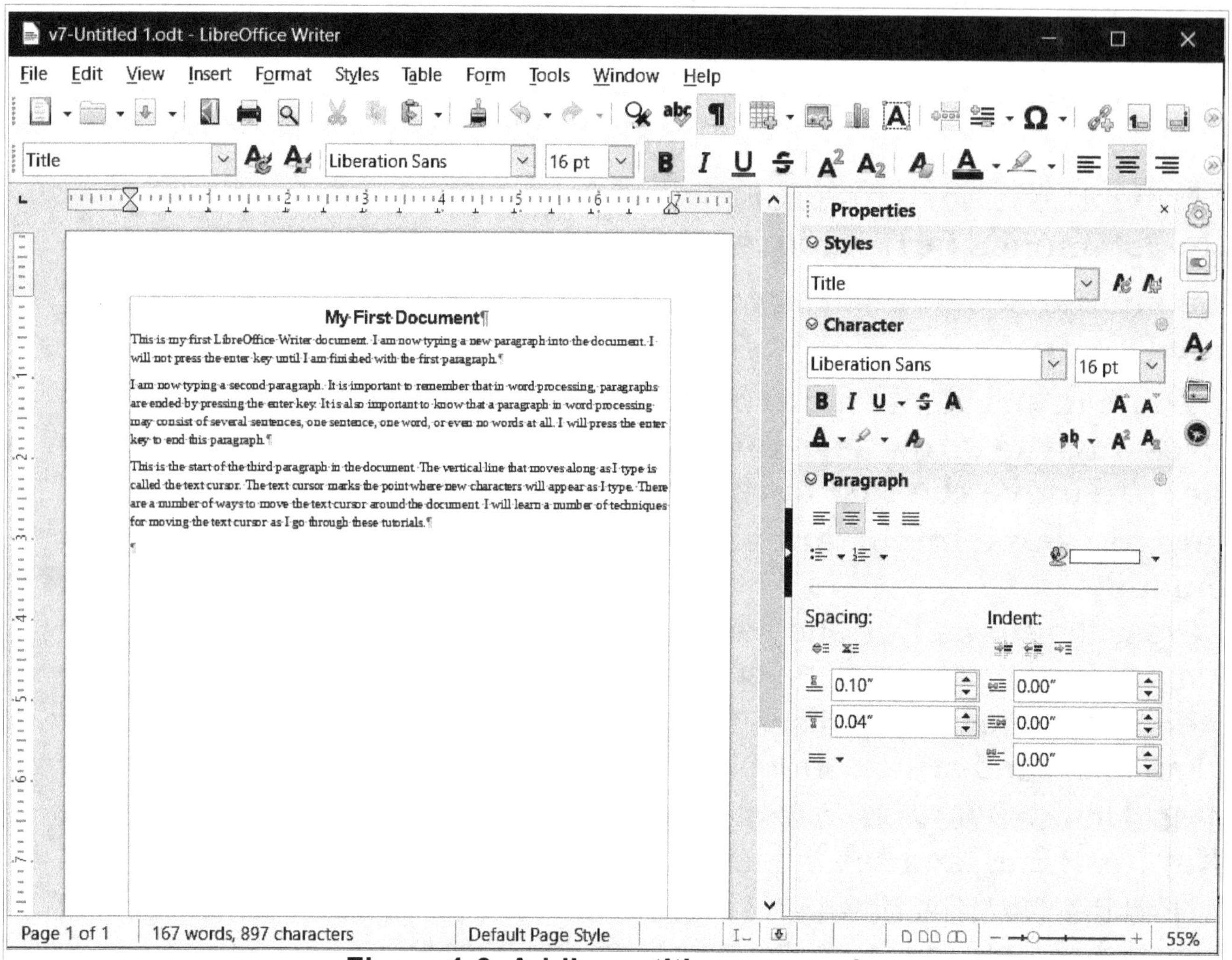

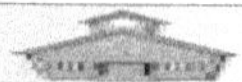

Figure 1-9, Adding a title paragraph.

Observe that the *TITLE* Paragraph Style has its own *font style, size, spacing*, and *alignment.*

Now that you have invested some time creating a document, it's time to take control of where it will be saved.

> **NOTE**: If you are already familiar with using *File Explorer* (or the similar function in Linux or Mac) go ahead and create a special location for the Practice document files. If not, please review **Appendix C**.

Saving a Document

✓ From the *Menubar*, select **File, Save As**.

✓ In the **Save As** dialog box, select the **C:** drive.

✓ Select the **New Folder** option, and enter **aaa My Practice Documents** as the folder name. (Adding aaa in front of the folder name is a trick for making the folder appear at the top of the list of folders.)

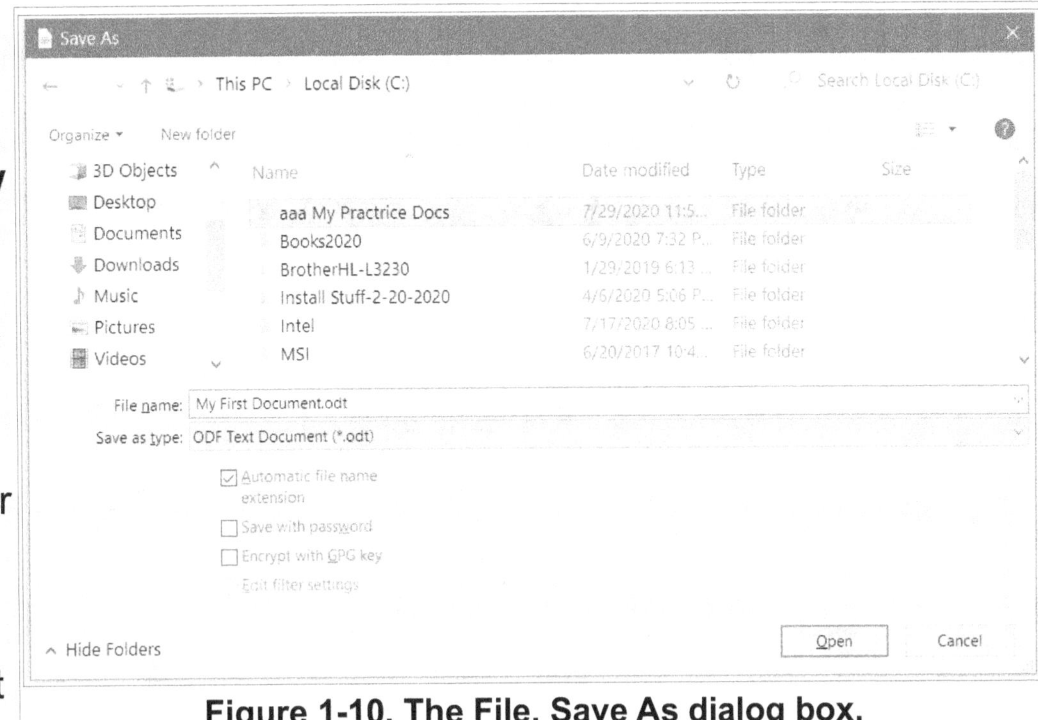

Figure 1-10, The File, Save As dialog box.

✓ **Open** the **aaa My Practice** documents folder and then enter **My First Document** as the file name.

Now you have prevented a blue bruise on your forehead if the power suddenly goes out, or if lighting strikes. You will know exactly where to find your document whenever you want to open it.

Before we leave this Project, let's take a quick look at some of the LibreOffice Writer display. features

LibreOffice Writer Display Features

At the bottom of the display you can see the *page count*, the *word count*, and the current *page style*.

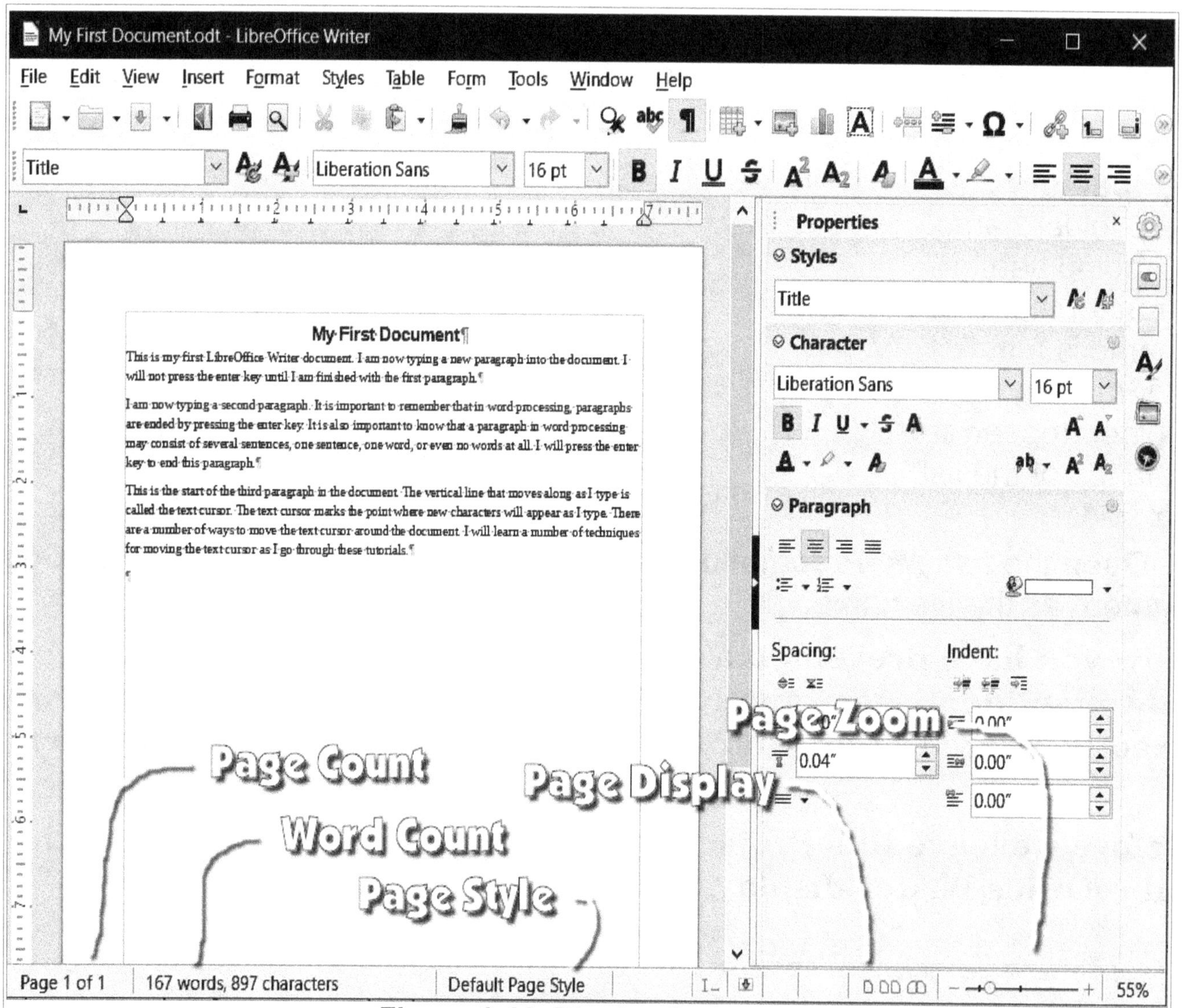

Figure 1-11, Display features.

You have already seen how to use *Paragraph Styles*. In a future lesson, you will learn the power of using *Page Styles.* Also in a future project, when you have many pages in your document, you will learn about the different *Page Display* options.

✔ The *Page Zoom* section has a couple of ways to make the page appear bigger or smaller without changing document font sizes. At the far right, the current ***zoom factor*** is displayed. There is a ***drag bar*** just to the left of the zoom factor that you can slide back and forth to change the zoom factor. You can also select the – or **+** at the ends of the drag bar to make small decreases or increased in the zoom factor. Try it…

Now it's time to practice.

✓ Close the ***My First Document*** file and re-start **LibreOffice**.

Go through ***all of the steps again***, but this time substitute your own text and file name.

Until you can start a new document on your own, repeat Project 1. Before long you will more and more comfortable with the tools and techniques covered in this lesson.

 **Project 2 ~ Creating an Illustrated Story** 

Introduction

In this project, you will learn how to create a multiple page story with graphic images inserted into the text. The sample story can be personalized by replacing the suggested text and pictures with your own selections.

> **NOTE**: This project assumes that you have completed Project 1. If you have not, you should do so first, otherwise some of the instructions may be confusing.

You should get into the habit of using *File, Save As* every time you start a new document. Otherwise you may find a bunch of *Untitled* documents in a mystery folder somewhere.

Creating a Story Document

✓ Open **LibreOffice** and start a new **Writer** document.

✓ Select **File, Save As**, set the **Save As** *folder* to your preferred location and enter **My Story** as the file name.

✓ Enter the text **MY Story** in the first paragraph in the document.

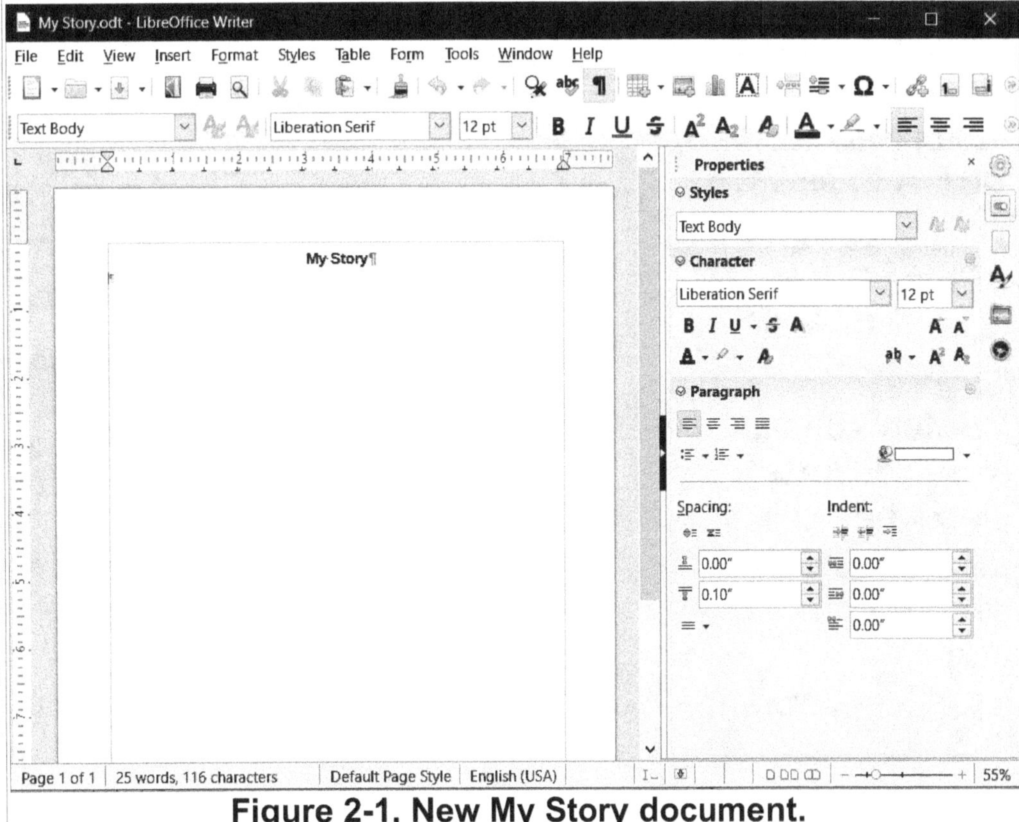

Figure 2-1, New My Story document.

✔ Before pressing the *Enter Key*, change the *Paragraph Style* to **TITLE**.

The text cursor should now be in the second paragraph and the *Paragraph Style* should show *Text Body*.

For the purpose of this project, we need to fill at least 4 pages of text. Four pages will provide the opportunity to learn about using page styles, including headers, and footers. You can enter your own text if you like. An alternative to entering your own text is to import some text called *Lorem Ipsum*, simulated text that has long been used by printers as placeholder text to aid in layouts and formatting. There are a number of Lorem Ipsum generators available on the Internet, Here is the address for one of them.

https://generator.lorem-ipsum.info

✔ Open the web page noted above.

✔ Place the cursor in the sample text box and then press **Ctrl+A** to select all the text.

✔ Press **Ctrl+C** to copy the selected text.

✔ Return to your story document, place the text cursor in the second paragraph.

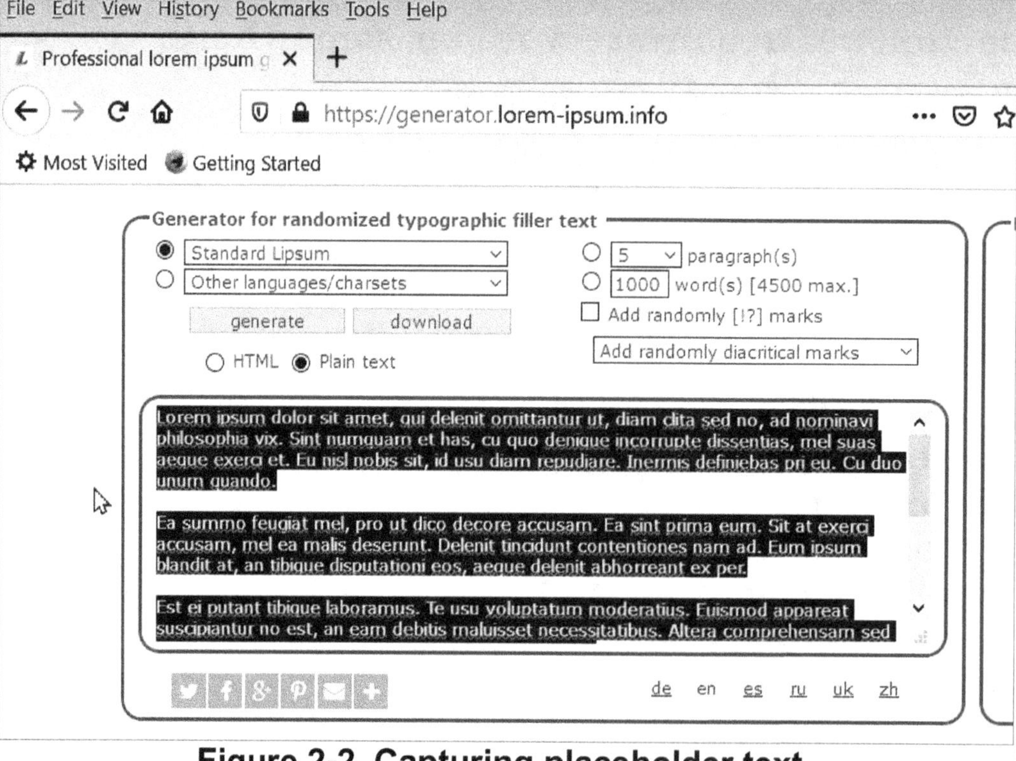

Figure 2-2, Capturing placeholder text.

✔ From the *Menubar*, select **Edit, Paste Special, Paste Unformatted Text**.

> **NOTE**: The combination of *Copy,* **Ctrl+C** and *Paste,* **Ctrl+V** is extremely powerful. You should memorized these key press shortcuts. When you want to take control of the text formatting in the copy, use **Edit, Paste Special, Paste Unformatted Text**.

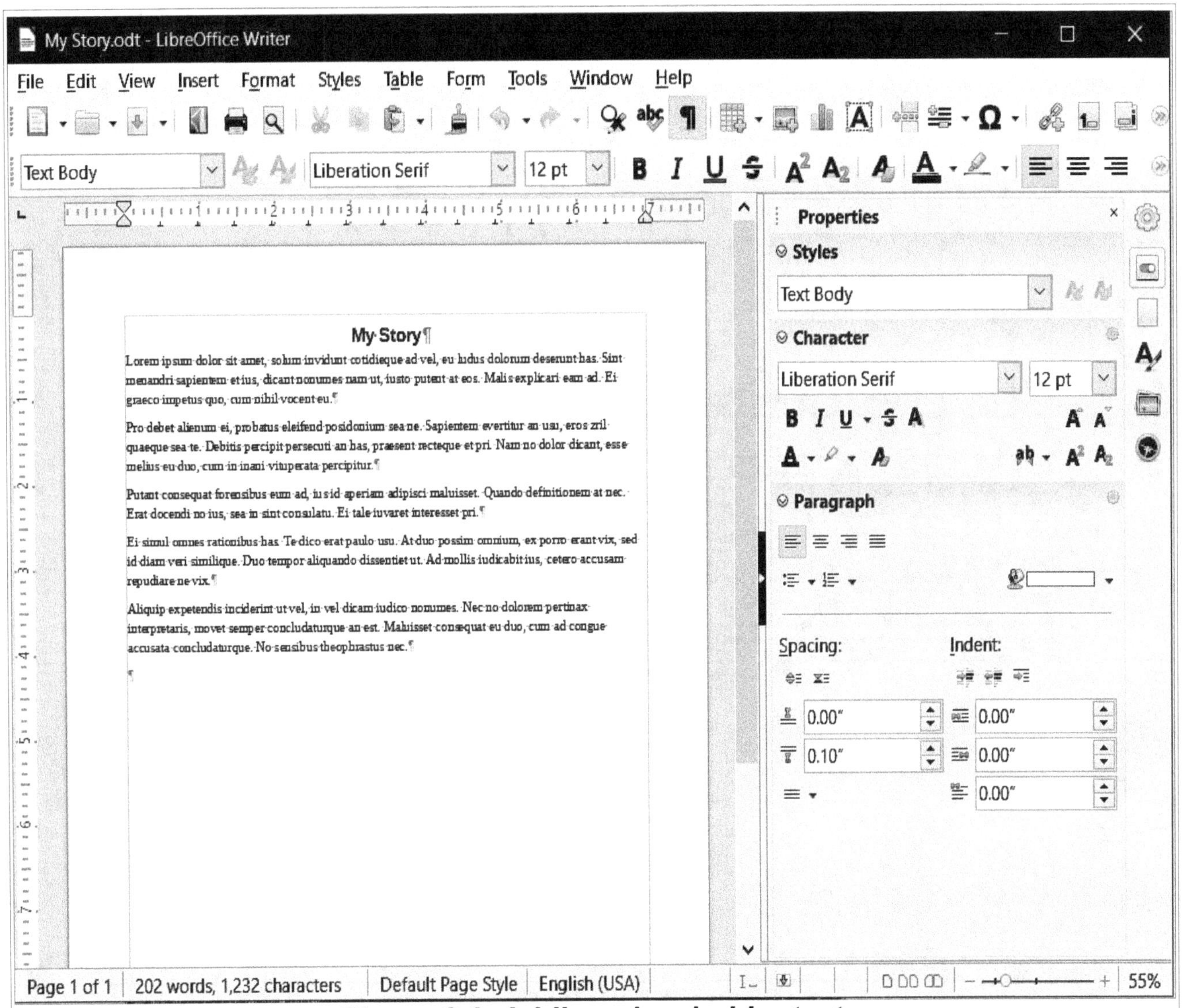

Figure 2-3, Adding placeholder text.

Figure 2-3 shows the result of pasting the placeholder text in the document. Notice that the extra unwanted blank paragraphs have been removed.

✔ Delete the unwanted blank paragraphs.

Next, a selection trick will be used to copy all of the text body paragraphs.

✔ ***Double click*** (press the ***left*** mouse button ***twice***) on the first word ***Lorem***.

✔ Hold the **Shift** key down, and then ***single click*** at the end of the last paragraph.

This should select all of the paragraphs.

✔ When all paragraphs have been selected, press **Ctrl+C** to copy them to the clipboard.

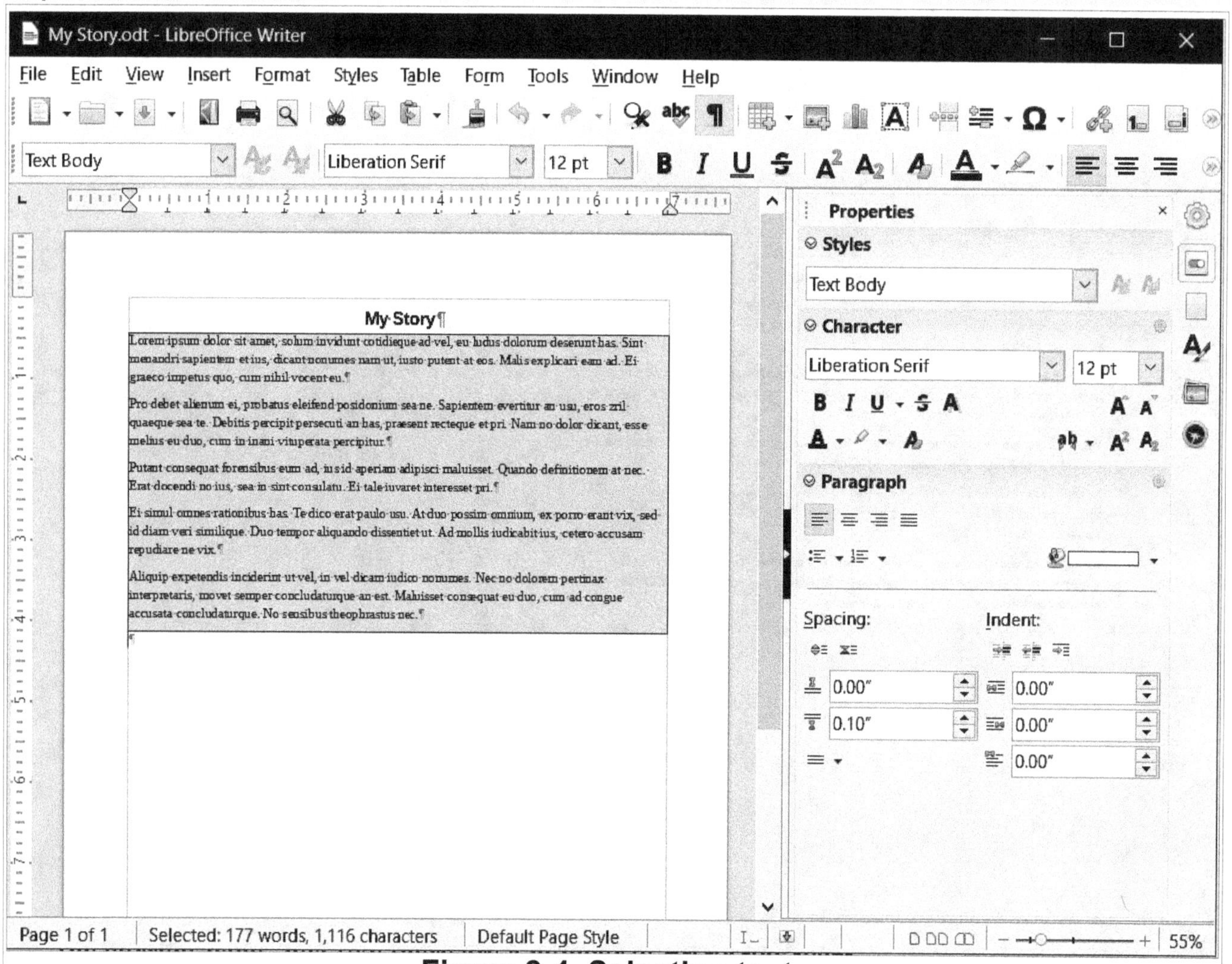

Figure 2-4, Selecting text.

✔ Place the text cursor ***below*** the last paragraph and press **Ctrl+V** to paste the copied text.

✔ Repeat pasting until the page count shows at least 4 pages.

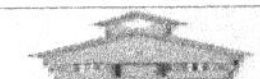

Observe that the bottom line of the display shows the *Page Style* of the current page. Just like there are a number of *Paragraph Styles* available, there are also different *Page Styles*.

- ✔ From the *Sidebar*, select the **Styles** option.
- ✔ Select the **Page Styles** tool.
- ✔ Check to make sure the *All Styles* list is shown.
- ✔ Place the text cursor somewhere in the *first page*.
- ✔ **Double click** on the **Right Page** option in the *Sidebar*.

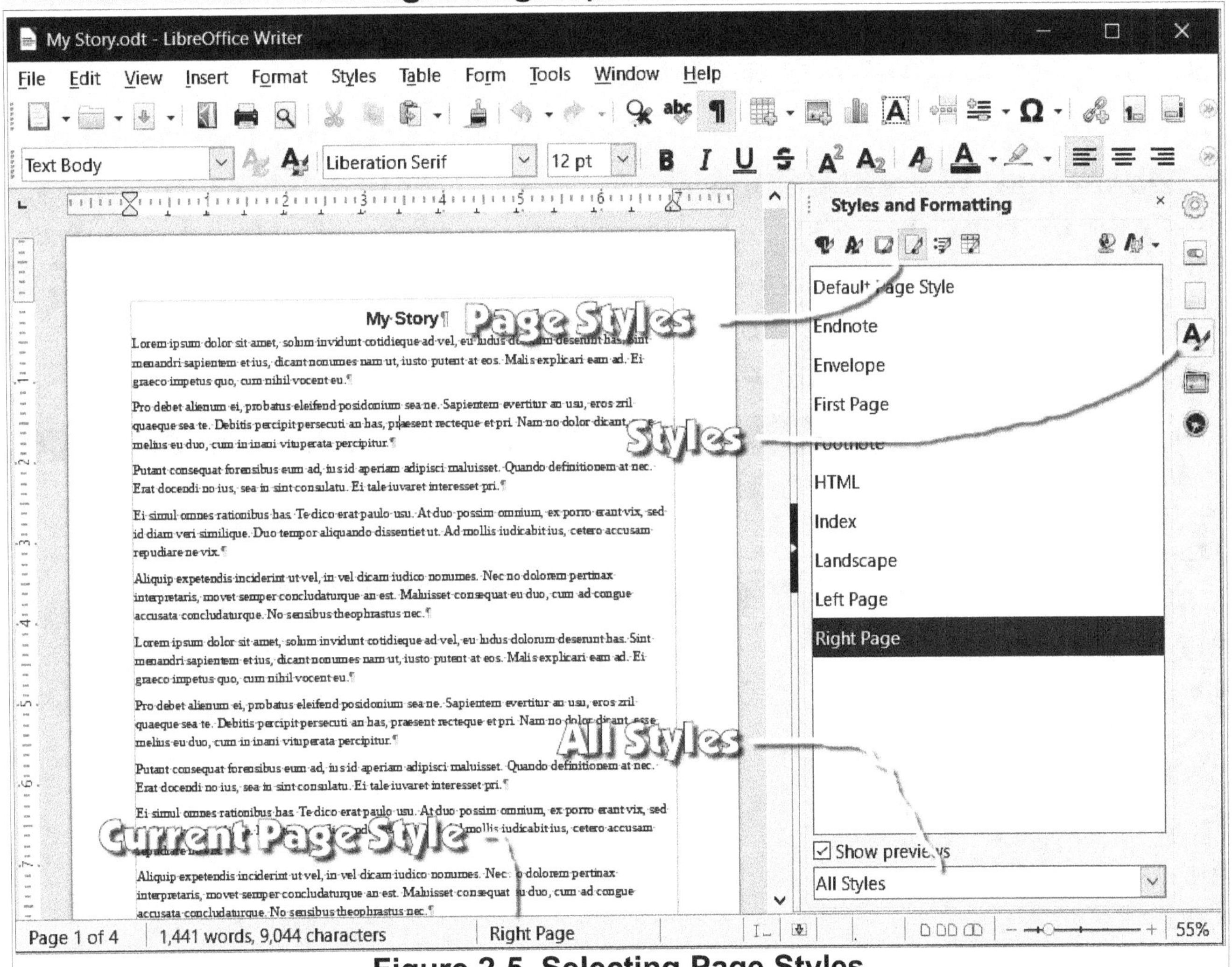

Figure 2-5, Selecting Page Styles.

When the text cursor is anywhere in Page 1, the *Page Style* indicator at the bottom of the display should show *Right Page*.

- ✔ Scroll down and place the text cursor some where in *Page 2*.

The *Page Style* indicator at the bottom of the display should show *Left Page*. Now, all of the odd numbered pages will be using the

Right Page style and all of the even pages will be using the *Left Page* style.

Each *Page Style* can be set to use a Page Style for the *next* page. In a more complicated document, perhaps a book, Page Styles can be set to have a cover page followed by a copyright page, followed by a contents page, followed by a chapter first page, and so on. This is powerful. Once page styles are set, all you have to do is keep entering text. The system will automatically manage Page Styles as you go.

Creating a Custom Page Style

Next, we will create our own custom page styles, *My Left Page*, and *My Right Page.* We will design the pages for double sided printing. This means that there should be a large margin (for binding) on the left side of right pages and on the right side for left pages.

  ✓ In the *Sidebar*, change the page style listing to **Custom**.

  ✓ *Right click* in the *Custom Page Style* list and select **New**.

  ✓ With the *Organizer* tab selected in the *Page Style* dialog box, enter **My Right Page** as the name and as the *Next* style.

We will change the next style after we create a My Left Page style.

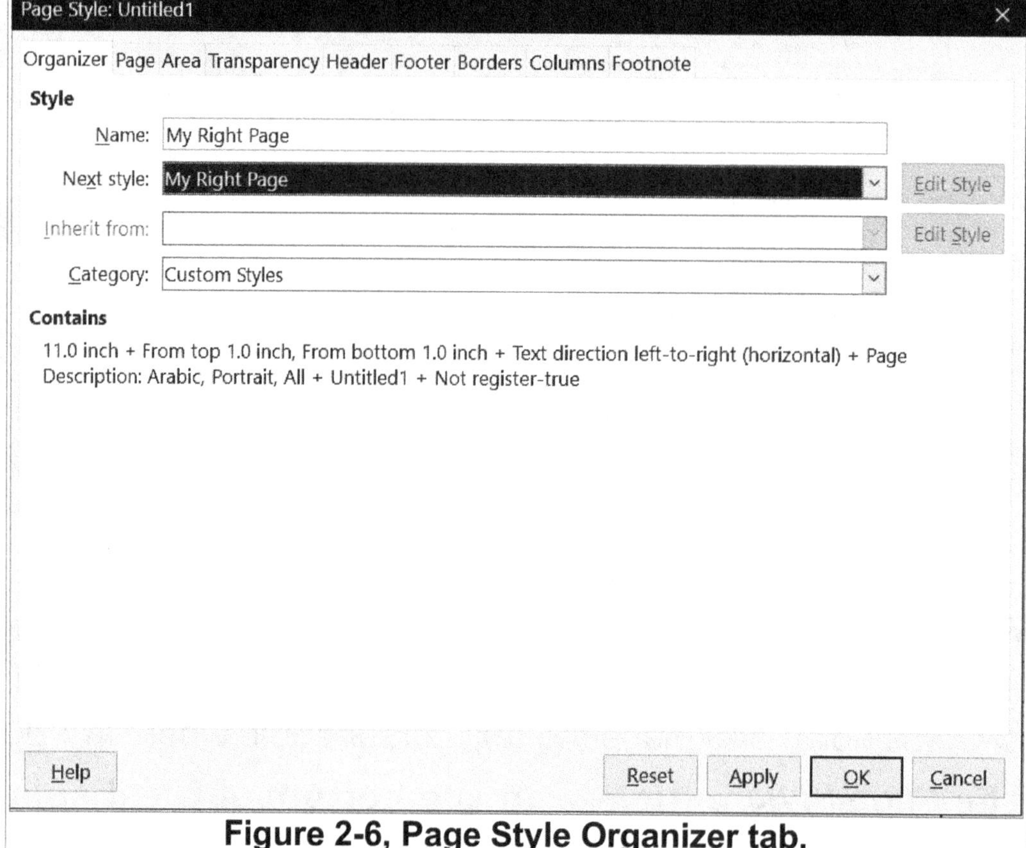

Figure 2-6, Page Style Organizer tab.

✓ Select the **Page** tab in the Page Style dialog box.

✓ Set the **Margins** as follows:

✓ **Left 0.75, Right 0.5, Top 0.5, Bottom 0.5.**

✓ Select the **Header** tab in the **Page Style** dialog box and toggle the **Header ON**.

✓ Select the **Footer** tab in the **Page Style** dialog box and toggle the **Footer ON**.

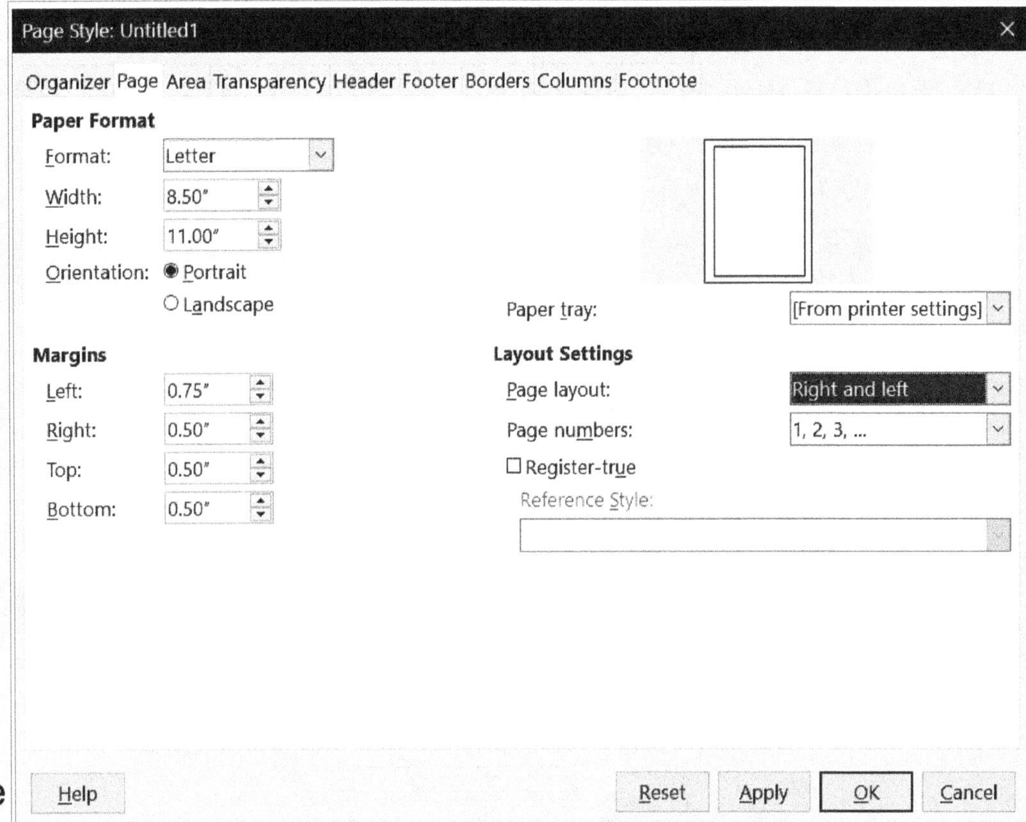

Figure 2-7, Setting page margins.

There are more Page Style settings, but this is all we need for now.

✓ Select **OK** to close the **Page Style** dialog box.

Next, we will repeat this process for a **My Left Page** style.

✓ **Right click** in the **Custom Page Style** list and select **New**.

✓ With the **Organizer** tab selected in the **Page Style** dialog box, enter **My Left Page** as the name and select **My Right Page** as the **Next** style.

✓ Select the **Page** tab in the **Page Style** dialog box.

✓ Set the **Margins** as follows:

✓ **Left 0.5, Right 0.75, Top 0.5, Bottom 0.5.**

✓ Select the **Header** tab in the **Page Style** dialog box and toggle the **Header ON**.

✓ Select the **Footer** tab in the **Page Style** dialog box and toggle the **Footer ON**.

✓ Select **OK** to close the **Page Style** dialog box.

✔ ***Right click*** on ***My Right Page*** style and select **Modify**.

Change the *Next* style to My Left Page.

Now we can use our new Page Styles on our document.

✔ Place the text cursor somewhere in ***Page 1***.

✔ ***Double click*** on **My Right Pag**e in the ***Sidebar***.

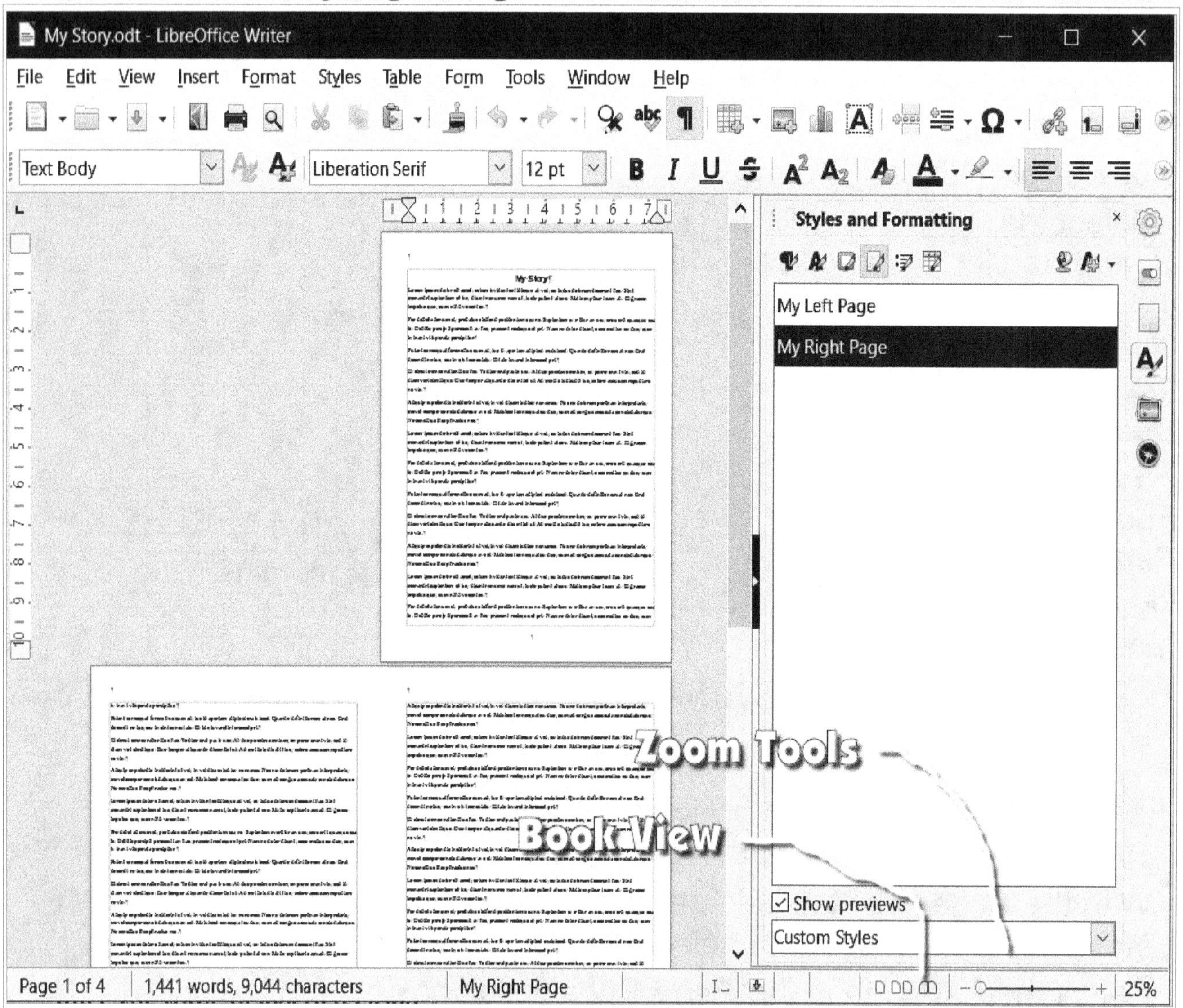

Figure 2-8, Book View.

As you scroll through the pages you can see the margins. This will be more obvious if you switch to ***Book View***.

✔ Select the **Book View** option and use the ***Zoom Tools*** to see how the book will appear when printed.

✔ Return to **Single page view** and adjust the ***Zoom***.

Have you saved your document lately?

Inserting Fields

Next, we will enter page numbers in the footers. This will introduce the topic of *Inserted Fields*.

✔ Place the text cursor in the Page 1 *footer*.

✔ Enter **Page** followed by a *space*.

✔ From the *Menubar*, select **Insert Field, Page Number**.

✔ Press the *Spacebar* enter **of**, press the *Spacebar*, and then select **Insert Field, Page Count.**

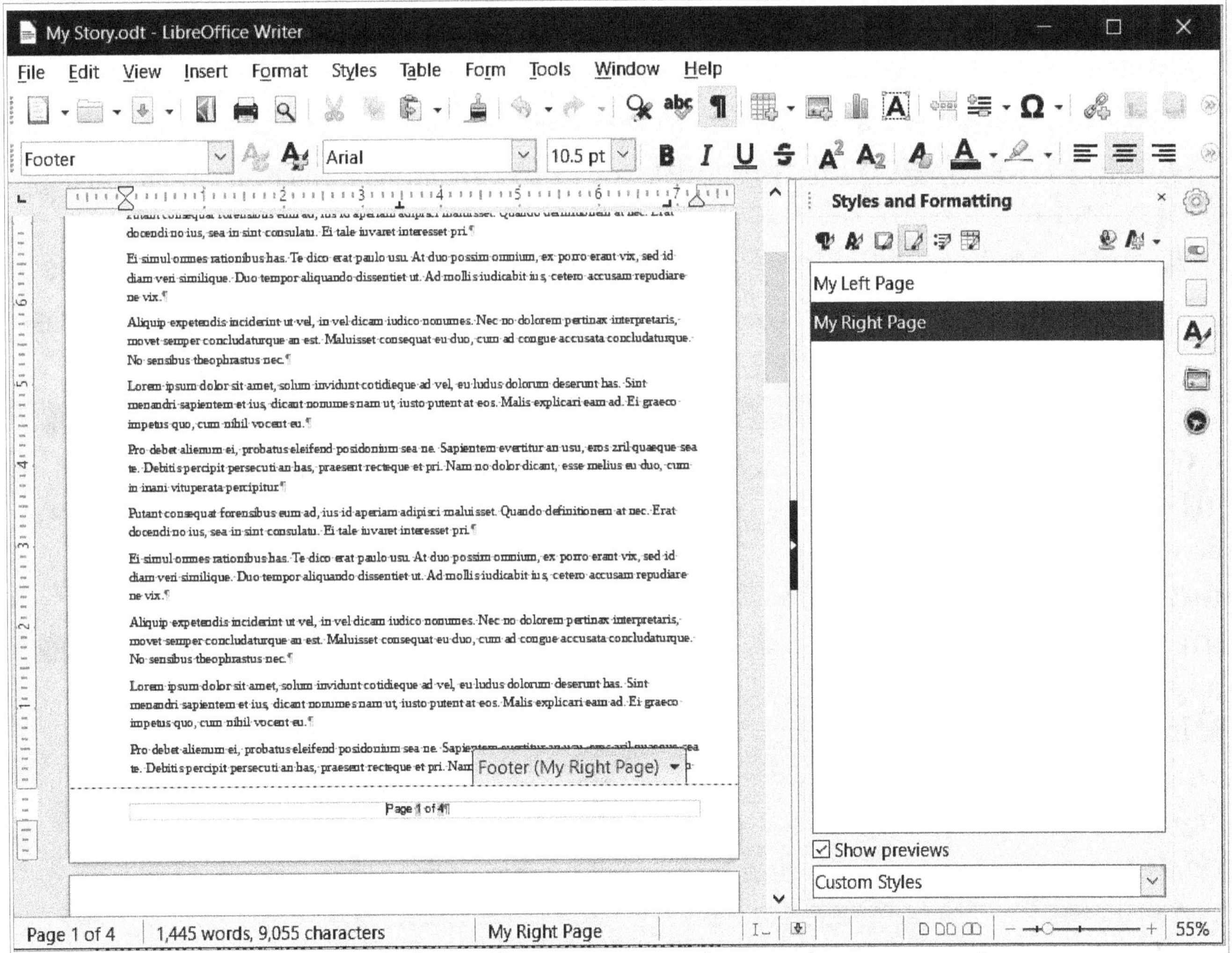

Figure 2-9, Inserting page number and page count.

✔ With the text cursor in the footer, select **Format, Aligned, Centered.**

Observe that *inserted fields*, in this case Page Number and Count, are displayed with shaded backgrounds. These backgrounds do not show up when the document is printed. The shading is a reminder that they are fields and cannot be edited.

Let's use the same footer for the Left Pages.

- ✓ Select all of the text in the right footer, Copy **Ctrl+C** and Paste **Ctrl+V** it into the left footer.
- ✓ With the text cursor in the footer, select **Format, Aligned, Centered**.

Next, lets add *headers* that use the *Title* field. First the *Title* has to be defined.

- ✓ From the *Menubar*, select **File, Properties**.
- ✓ With the *Description* tab selected in the *Properties* dialog box, enter **My Story**, as the **Title**, then select **OK**.
- ✓ Place the text cursor in the Page 2 header and select **Insert, Field, Title**.
  - ✓ With the text cursor in the header, select **Format, Aligned, Centered**.

The title will now automatically appear in every even page header. If you want to change the Title, just edit the title Property and every header on every even numbered (or left) page will automatically be updated.

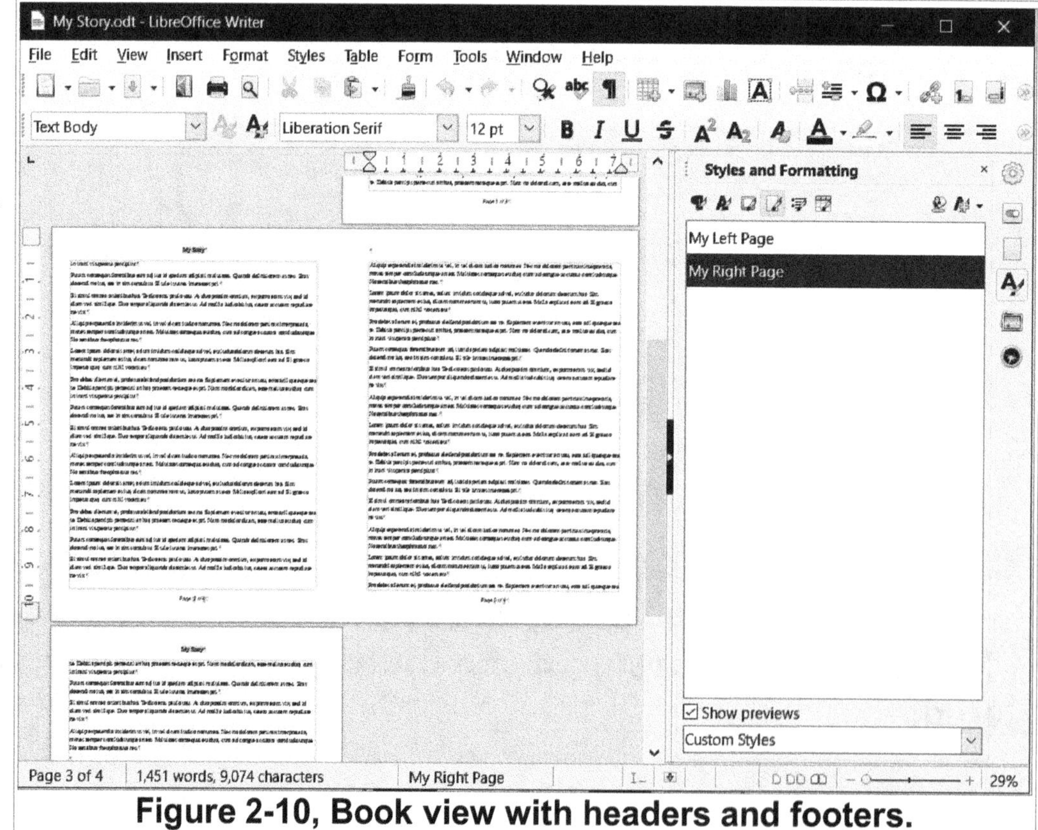

Figure 2-10, Book view with headers and footers.

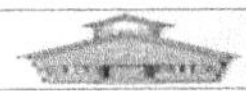

You can create custom Paragraph Styles for headers and footers that include special fonts, borders, background fills, and even graphic images like the ones in this book. The great thing is that you only have to create the styles once and they are automatically applied to the entire document. Try to do that with your old IBM Selectric.

BTW Have you saved your document lately? Never spend more time between saves then you are willing to repeat if something goes wrong. I predict that you will sometime get a blue bruise on your forehead because you failed to save often.

Inserting Images

Graphics files (pictures, drawings, and other images) can be inserted into documents, or into frames within documents. They can either be embedded or linked. It is not possible to tell the difference between embedded and linked graphics by simply looking at a document.

Embedded graphics become an integral part of the document and increase the size of the file.

Linked graphics are not added directly to a document. Instead, the document contains a pointer, or file address, that the system uses to fetch the file whenever it is needed.

An advantage of linked files is that if the original graphic is changed, the document will automatically include the changed graphic. Also, by linking graphics, the document size is smaller than it would be if the graphic was embedded.

A disadvantage of linked graphics is that if the document is moved from one computer to another, the linked files must also be moved. The trick to solving this problem is to create a special folder for the document with a graphics sub-folder. If the document folder is copied to a different computer, the linked files folder will follow along. Not linking files removes this problem, but increases file size.

We will insert an image in the first page and have the text wrap around the image.

Place the text cursor somewhere in the first paragraph.

✔ From the **Menubar**, select **Insert, Image**.

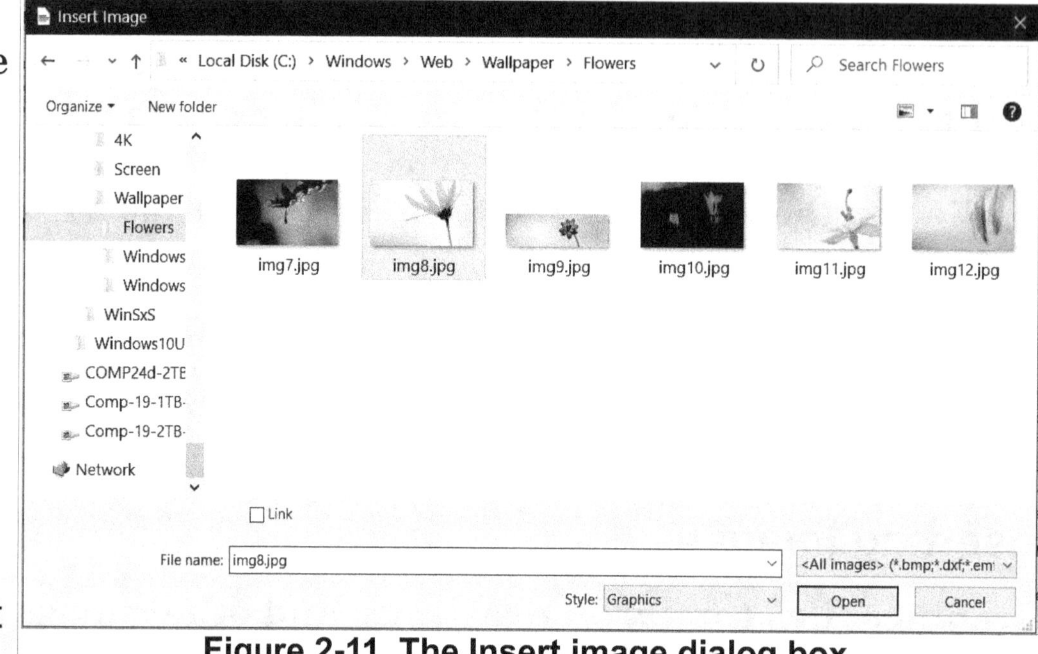

Figure 2-11, The Insert image dialog box.

[You can also use the **Insert Image** tool on the **Toolbar**.]

This opens the *Insert image* dialog box. You can select any picture. Figure 2-11 shows images from *Local Disk (C:), Windows, Web, Wallpaper, Flowers*.

✔ Select an image and then select **Open**.

✔ **Double click** on the inserted image.

This will open the *Image* dialog box. Note that this dialog box has a number of tabs for different settings.

✔ Select the **Type** tab in the *Image* dialog box.

✔ Toggle the **Keep ratio** option **ON**.

✔ Set the **Width** to **2.50**.

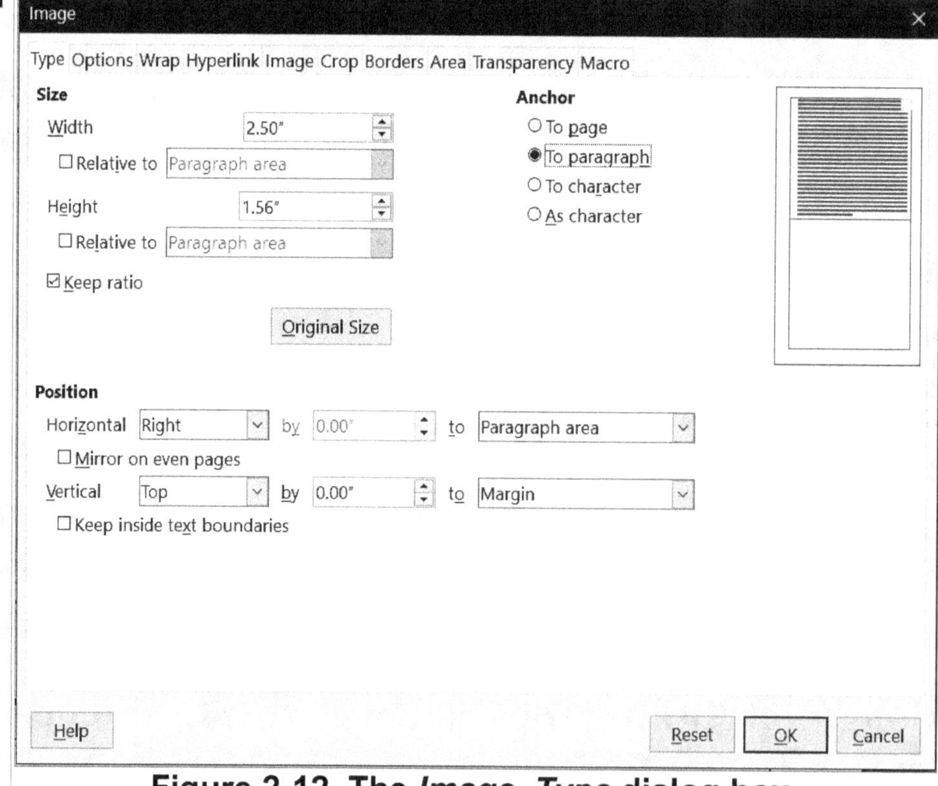

Figure 2-12, The *Image, Type* dialog box.

✔ Set the **Anchor To** **paragraph**.

✔ Set the *Horizontal* position to **Right**.

Next, the *Wrap* options will be set.

✔ Select the **Wrap** tab in the *Image* dialog box.

✔ Select the **Before** option.

✔ Set *Spacing* to **0.02** for all sides.

Next, the *Border* options will be set.

✔ Select the **Border** tab in the *Image* dialog box.

✔ Select the **All four borders** option.

✔ Select **OK**.

Observe that the Borders tab has options for selecting a line style and adding a shadow.

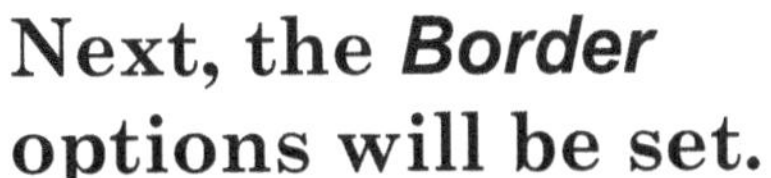

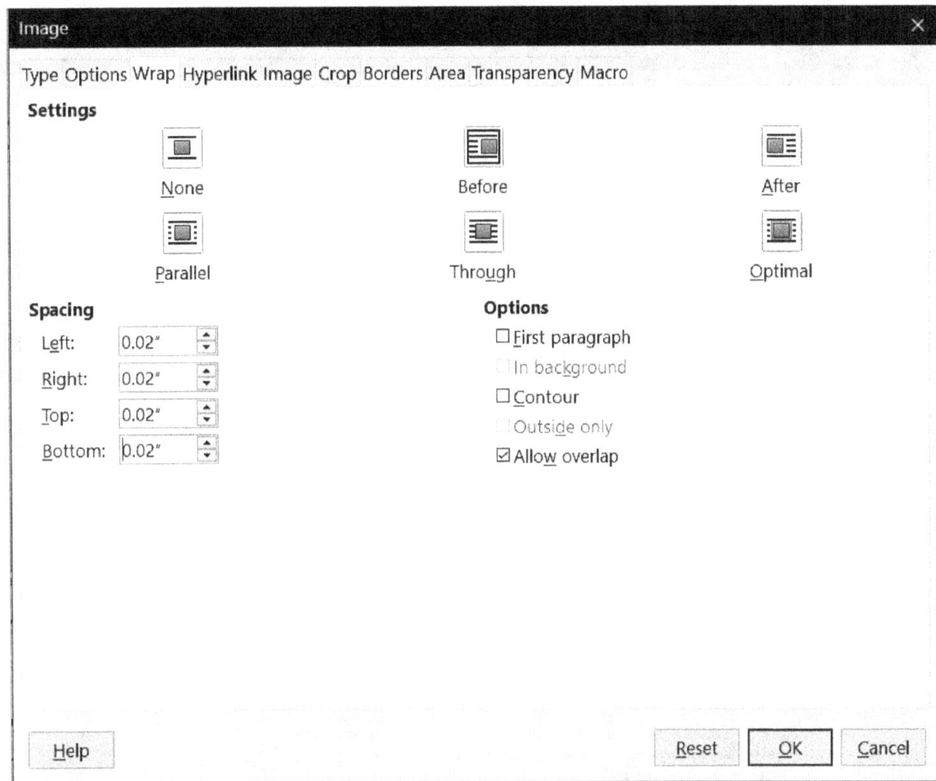

Figure 2-13, Setting Image, Wrap options.

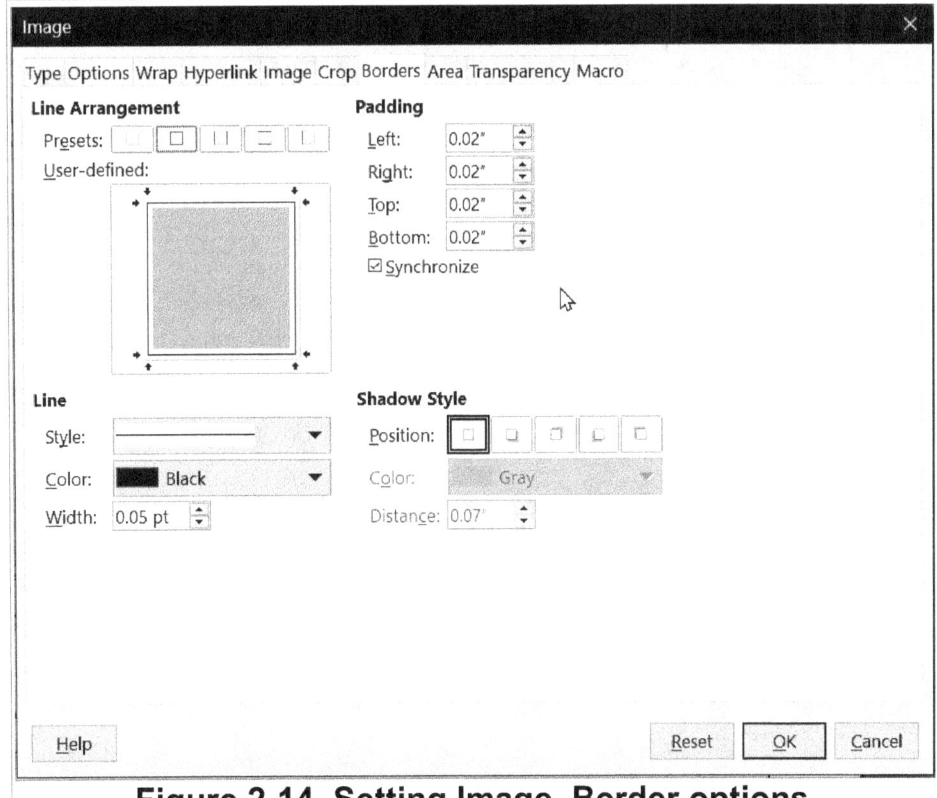

Figure 2-14, Setting Image, Border options.

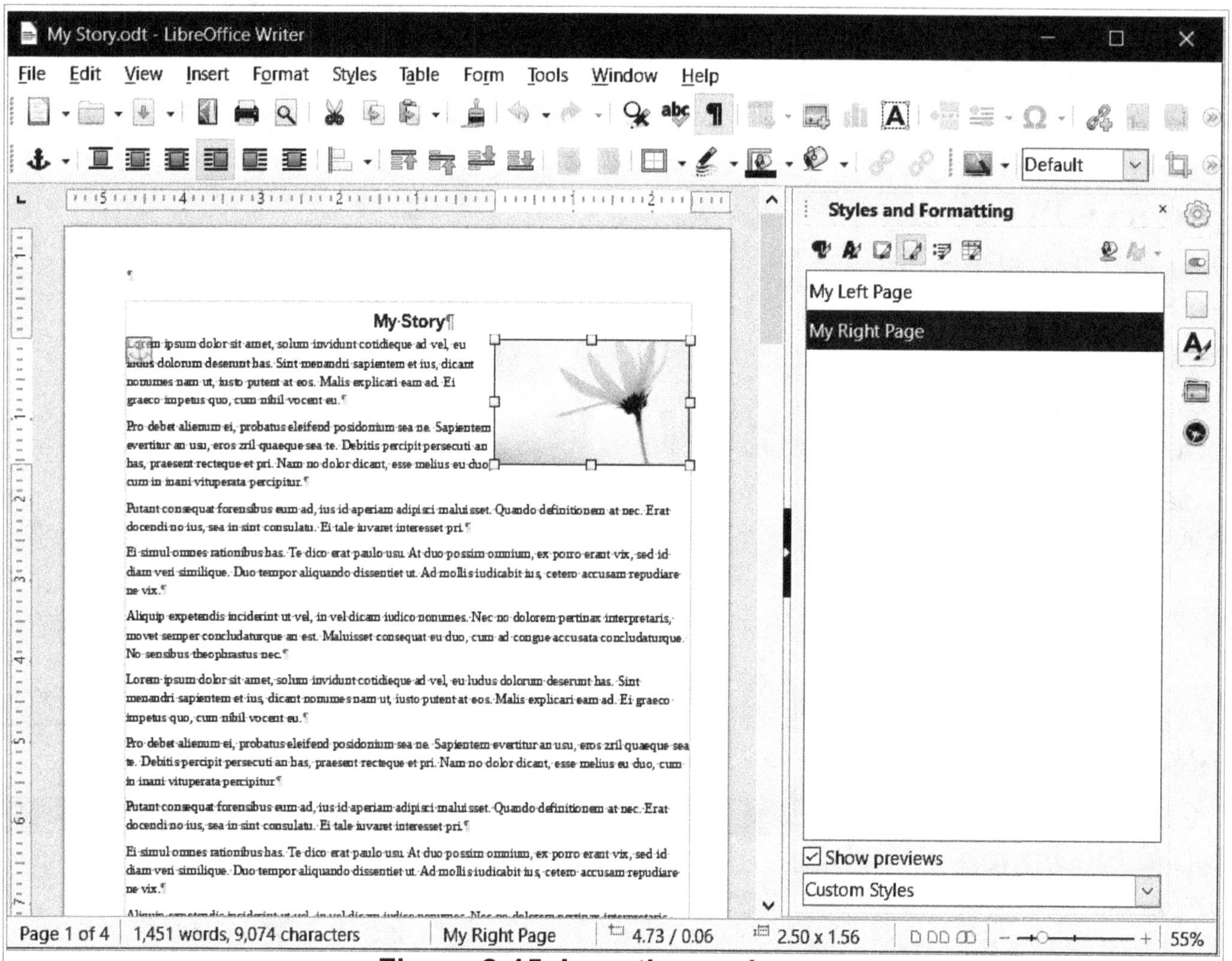

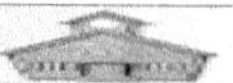

Figure 2-15, Inserting an image.

Your document should now look similar to Figure 2-15.

✓ You should now experiment with inserting images in your document. Try the different **Wrap** options. Observe the different **Border** options.

Copy and Paste Images

Remember the powerful *Copy* and *Paste* trick? It turns out that you can use Copy and Paste to insert images. Here is an example.

✓ Open your web browser to **Google Images** and enter **Tree** in the search box.

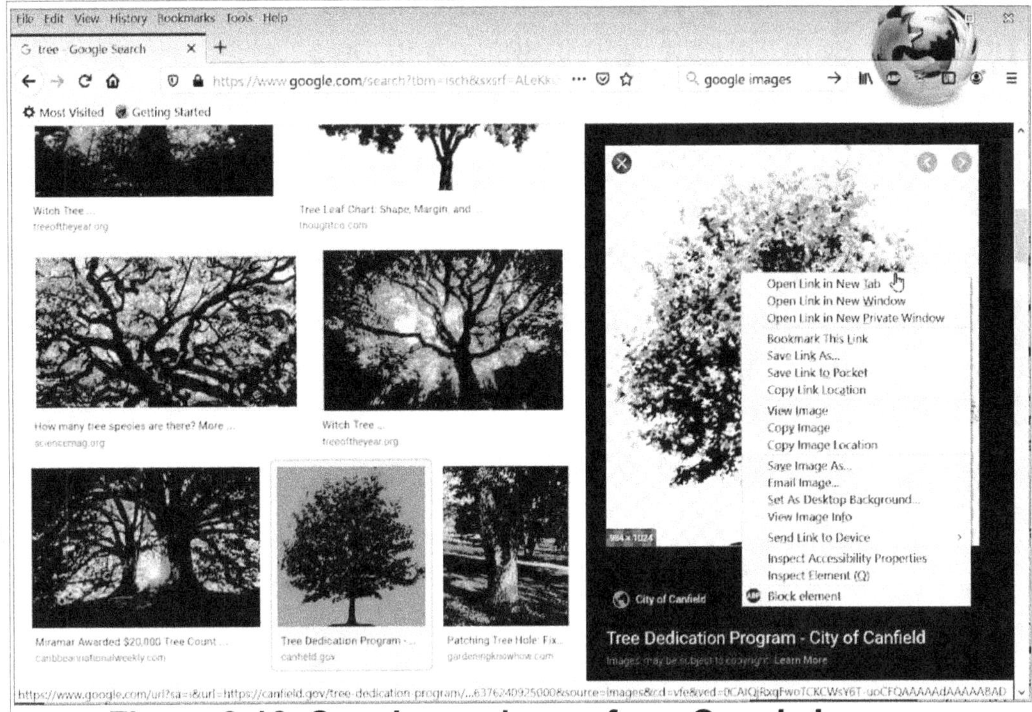

Figure 2-16, Copying an image from Google Images.

✓ Select a tree by **left clicking** on the thumbnail image, and then **right click** on the tree image in the side panel.

✓ Select **Copy Image** from the pop up context menu.

✓ Place the text cursor on page 2 of your document/

✓ **Paste** the image (**Ctrl+V**).

✓ **Double click** on the image and adjust the image settings as desired.

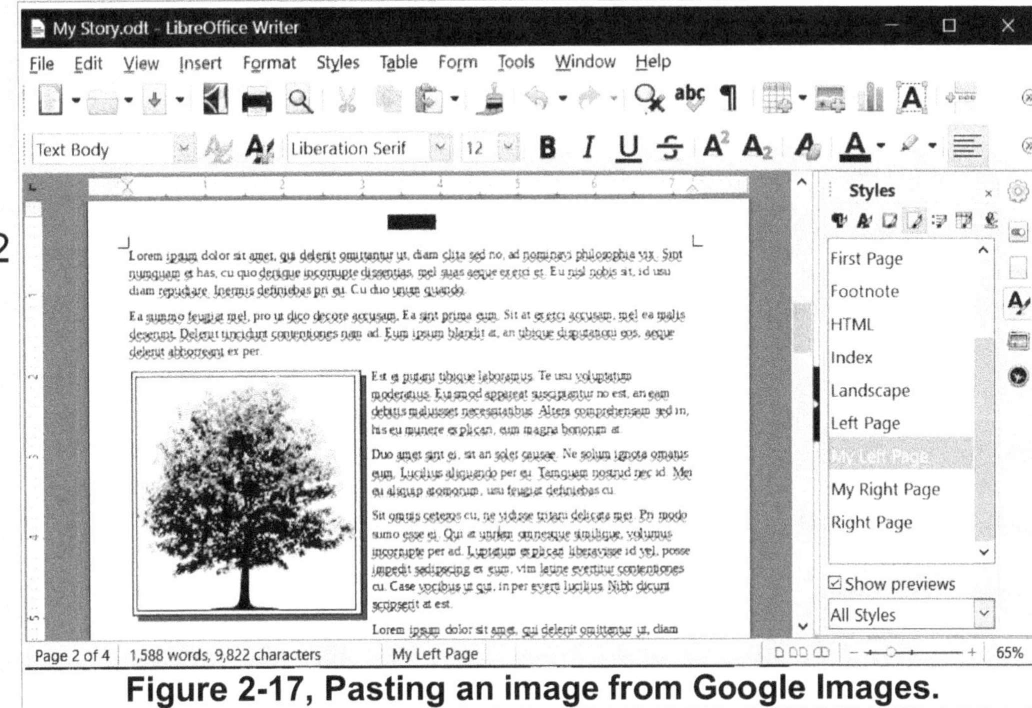

Figure 2-17, Pasting an image from Google Images.

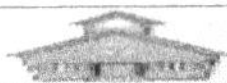

As you can see, it's easy to enhance your documents by inserting images.

 ✔ You should **save** your document with a ***new name*** to preserve the original, and then experiment with inserting images.

It's time to practice. Close LibreOffice and go back to the beginning of this Project and do it again. Create your own story title and text. This time try to observe the different options in the various dialog boxes. Don't be afraid to experiment.

When you become comfortable with creating the practice project, create your own multiple page story from scratch. You now have the tools to create professional appearing documents that will amaze and surprise your friends.

Creating a Family History Book

This lesson covers the basics of creating a multi-chapter book. If you have completed Projects 1 and 2, you already know most of what you need to know to create books. However, a book requires a lot of planning and organizing. You need to decide on where the different parts of the book will be saved. You also need to make decisions about the page and paragraph styles to be used.

The formats and styles presented here follow the requirements for preparing a book that can be published on Amazon using kdp (Kindle Desktop Publishing) guidelines, or on other self-publishing web sites. This project requires that you have already completed Projects 1 and 2 earlier in this book.

Organize Files

You should organize your book files in a special folder with sub folders for graphics files.

✓ Create a folder named **My Book**. In the My Book folder, create a folder named **My Book Graphics Files**. There will also be odt files for each chapter, and another odt file named **My Book Project**.

We will create an odt file named **My Book Base** that we will use to save all of the custom page and paragraph styles for the book.

Required Custom Styles

Planning a book for publication requires decisions on what page and paragraph styles will be required. Books might include the following *Page Styles*:

- Title Page
- Copyright Page
- Contents Page, or Pages
- Right Page
- Left Page

The following *Paragraph Styles* will be needed:

- Book Title
- Chapter Title

> Heading Paragraph
> Text Body
> Header
> Footer

Some authors might include special paragraph styles for large quotations, poems, or other special formatting. Perhaps you would like different header and footer styles for left and right pages.

The following example will establish styles for a typical 6 by 9 inch book.

Creating Page Styles

✓ Open a new *LibreOffice Writer* document.

✓ Select *File, Save As*, and create a *folder* named **My Book Project**. Save the new file as **My Book Base**.

This file will be used to start each new book chapter.

In this project, custom page styles for a 6×9 book will be created. This is a common paperback book size. You can substitute any book size you prefer. First, any existing custom styles will be removed. This will provide complete control of styles and avoid any inherited default styles.

✓ Set the *Sidebar* to display *Styles and Formatting*.

✓ Select the *Custom Styles* option.

✓ Select the *Paragraph* tool. If there are any Custom Style paragraphs listed select the first one, select **Ctrl+A** to select all, *right click* and select **Delete**.

✓ Repeat this for *Character, Frame, Page, List,* and *Table* styles.

✓ **Save** the document.

You should now have a clean blank document to work with. Next, some custom *Page Styles* will be created.

✓ In the *Styles and Formatting Sidebar*, be sure *Custom Styles* are selected, then select the **Page** option.

✓ *Right click*, select **New** and enter **My Left Page** in the *Organizer* TAB.

✓ Make the *Next Page* be *My Left Page*.

The next page will be changed to My Right Page, after that style has been created.

✔ Select the *Page TAB*, set the *Width* to **6.00** and the *Height* to **9.00**.

✔ Set the *margins* as follows; **Left 0.60**, **Right 0.76**, **Top** and **Bottom 0.50**.

Since we are creating a document to be printed on two sides of the pages, the *right* margin will be **0.76** for left side pages and the *left* margin will be **0.76** for right side pages.

✔ Turn **on** *Headers* and *Footers*., then select **OK** to close the dialog box.

✔ Repeat the above process to create **My Right Page**. Make the next page be *My Left Page*.

✔ Set the page properties the same as for My Left Page except make the **Left** margin **0.76** and the *Right* margin to **0.60**.

✔ Set the *Header* and *Footer* to **ON**.

✔ *Right click* on *My Left Pag*e, select **Modify**, and set the next page to *My Right Page*.

Next, two contents pages will be created. If you do not want to include a list of contents in your book, you may skip these.

✔ *Right click* in the *Custom Page Styles Sidebar,* select **New** and enter **My Contents 2 Page** in the *Organizer* TAB.

✔ Select **My Right Page** as the *next page*.

✔ Set the page properties the same as *My Left Page*.

Repeat this for a second contents page.

✔ *Right click* in the *Custom Page Styles Sidebar,* select **New** and enter **My Contents 1 Page** in the *Organizer* TAB.

✔ Select **My Contents 2 Page** as the *next page*.

✔ Set the page properties the same as *My Right Page*.

Next, a Copyright page will be created. This page will be on the back of the Title Page, and will be on the left side of the open book.

✔ *Right click* in the *Custom Page Styles Sidebar,* select **New** and enter **My Copyright Page** in the *Organizer* TAB.

✔ Select **My Contents 1 Page** as the *next page*.

✔ Set the page properties the same as *My Left Page*.

Finally, the Title Page will be created.

✔ *Right click* in the *Custom Page Styles Sidebar,* select **New** and enter **My Title Page** in the *Organizer* TAB.

✓ Select **My Copyright Page** as the *next page*.

✓ Set the page properties the same as *My Right Page,* except do not turn the header and footer on.

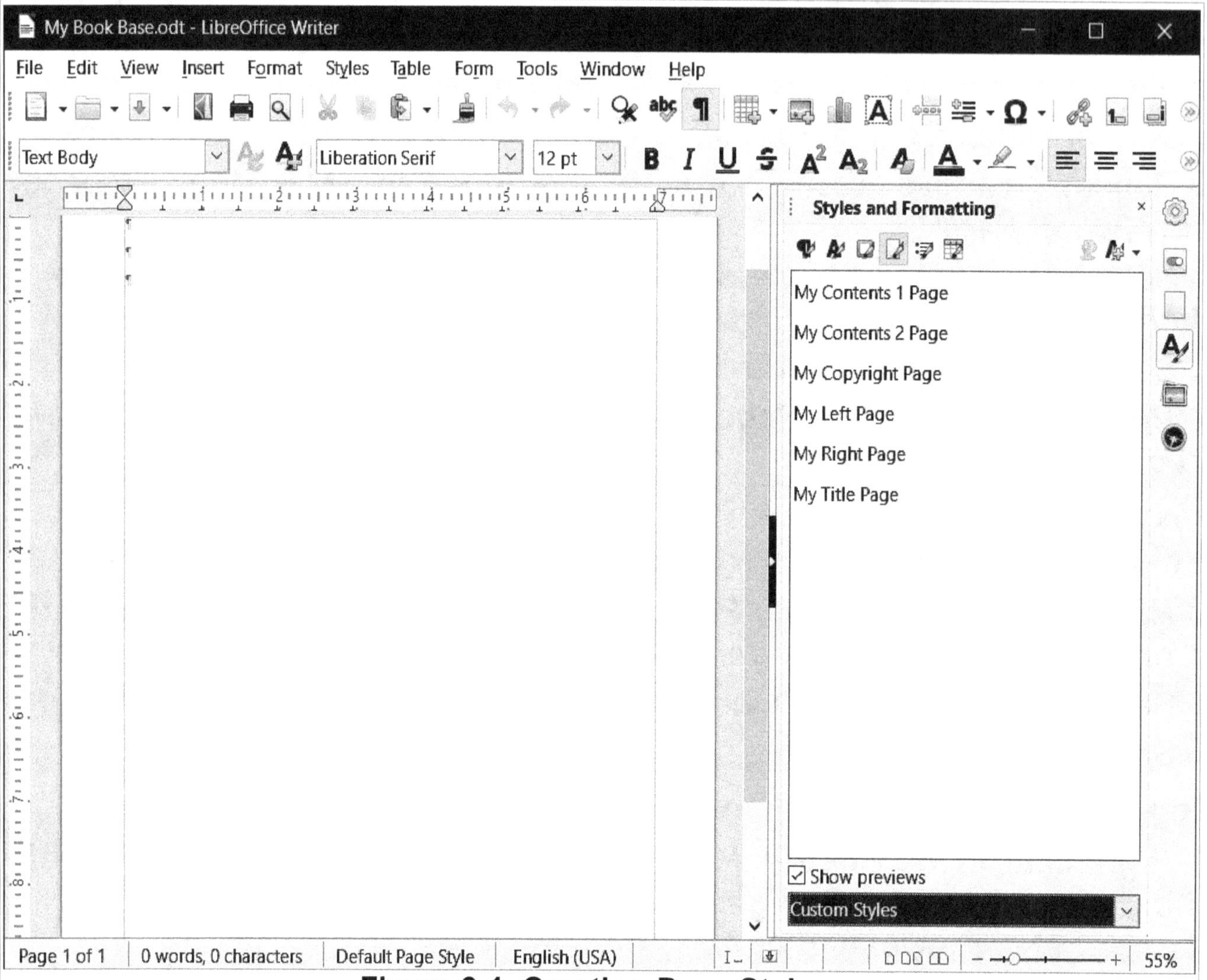

Figure 3-1, Creating Page Styles.

Next, the custom paragraph styles will be created. At a minimum, you will need paragraph styles for the *text body* and *chapter titles*. You might also want special styles for the *copyright page text*, and perhaps for a *book title* and *author.*

✓ Set the *Sidebar* to display *Styles and Formatting* and select the *Paragraph* tool.

✓ *Right click* in the *Custom Styles* area and select **New**.

✓ In the *Organizer* tab, enter **My Text Body**. Set My Text Body as the **Next** paragraph style.

✓ Select *Inherit* from to **None**.

Now, you have to make decisions about the body text. Perhaps most important is the font style and size. This will depend on the audience for your book. For most adults, 14 point type is recommended, especially for older adults. You have to decide between serif and sans serif, and the spacing between lines and paragraphs.

Don't worry too much about this decision. With LibreOffice Writer, it is easy to change paragraph styles for the whole book with just a few mouse clicks.

> Baskerville 14 serif
>
> Bookman Old Style 14
>
> Times New Roman 14
>
> **Liberation Serif 14**
>
> **Liberation Sans 14**
>
> **Figure 3-2: Sample fonts.**

Note: To see what fonts are available on a Windows 10 computer, Select; **This PC, C:, Windows, Fonts.**

✓ In the **Paragraph Style** dialog box, choose spacing, text flow (hyphenation, Widows, and Orphans) font, and other preferred settings.

✓ *Right click* in the **Custom Styles** area and select **New**.

✓ Create **My Chapter Title Paragraph**, **My Copyright Paragraph**, **My Title Paragraph** and **My Heading 1 Paragraph** styles.

✓ Create **My Header Paragraph** and **My Footer Paragraph** styles.

If you want different header and footer alignments on odd and even pages, you will need *My Left* and *My Right* header and footer styles.

NOTE: The *My Heading 1 Paragraph* style is optional. It is used for sub sections of the book. If you want to incorporate a *Table of Contents* in your book, the *My Heading 1 Paragraphs* will appear in the *Table of Contents*.

✓ Press **Ctrl+Home** to place the cursor in the first line, and *double click* on **My Title Paragraph**.

✓ Select the *Page* tool and double click on **My Title Page**.

✓ Enter some sample text and test the different paragraph styles..

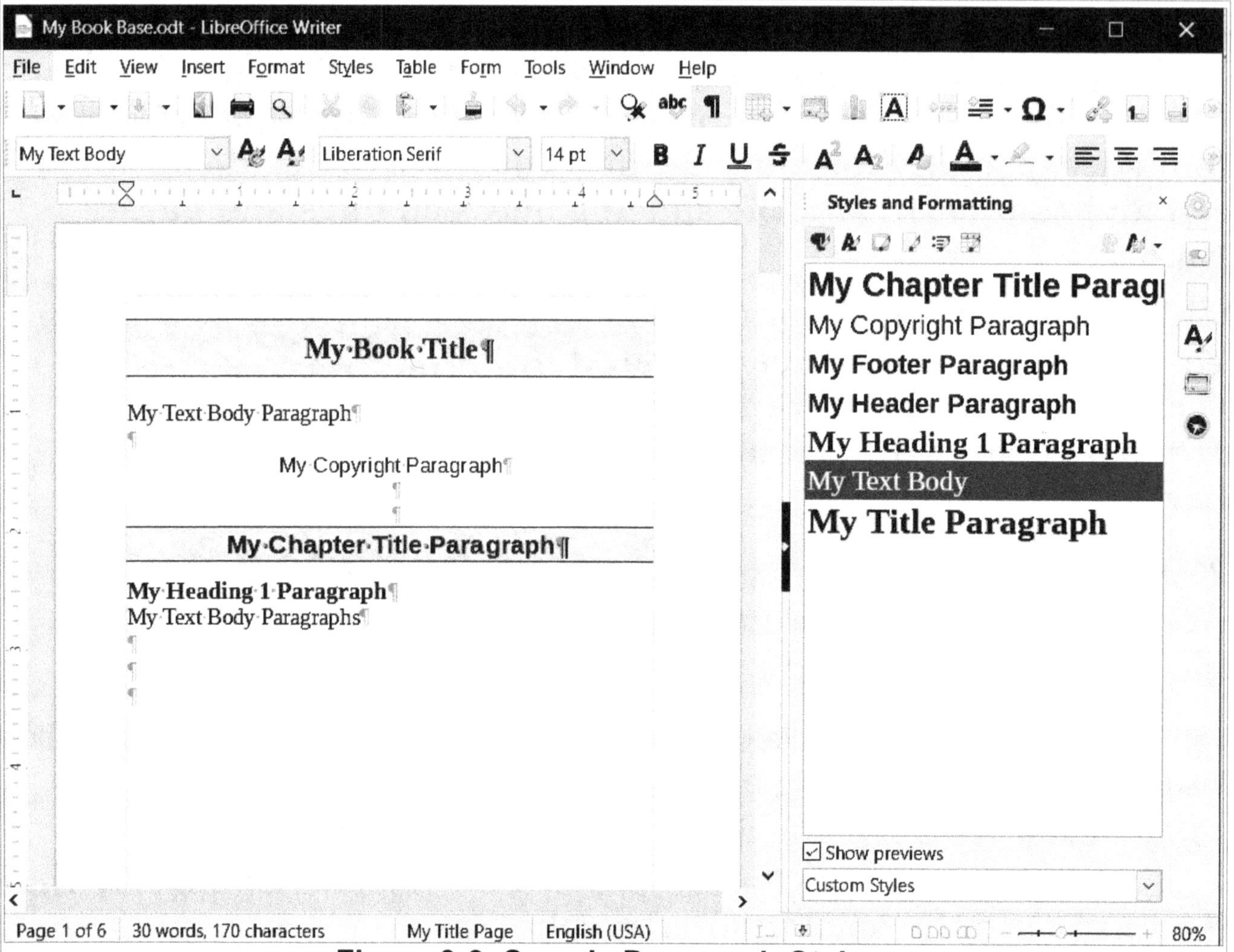

Figure 3-3, Sample Paragraph Styles.

Figure 3-3 shows some possible paragraph styles. You have the power to create your own styles. In the example shown, the *Book Title* and *Chapter Title* paragraphs have a bitmap *Area* fill. They have a border above and below. The *Title* paragraph has some *padding* added above and below the border text.

✓ At this point, it is a good idea to check your book page layout. Set **My Title Page** as the page style for the first page. Force a page break by pressing **Ctrl+Enter**.

✓ Put some sample text on the page and force another page break. Repeat this until you have at least 6 pages.

✓ Select the **Book View** option, in the lower right corner of the display, and adjust the Zoom to see how the book layout appears. If

you have missed any page style settings, it will be obvious. This is
the time to fix things.

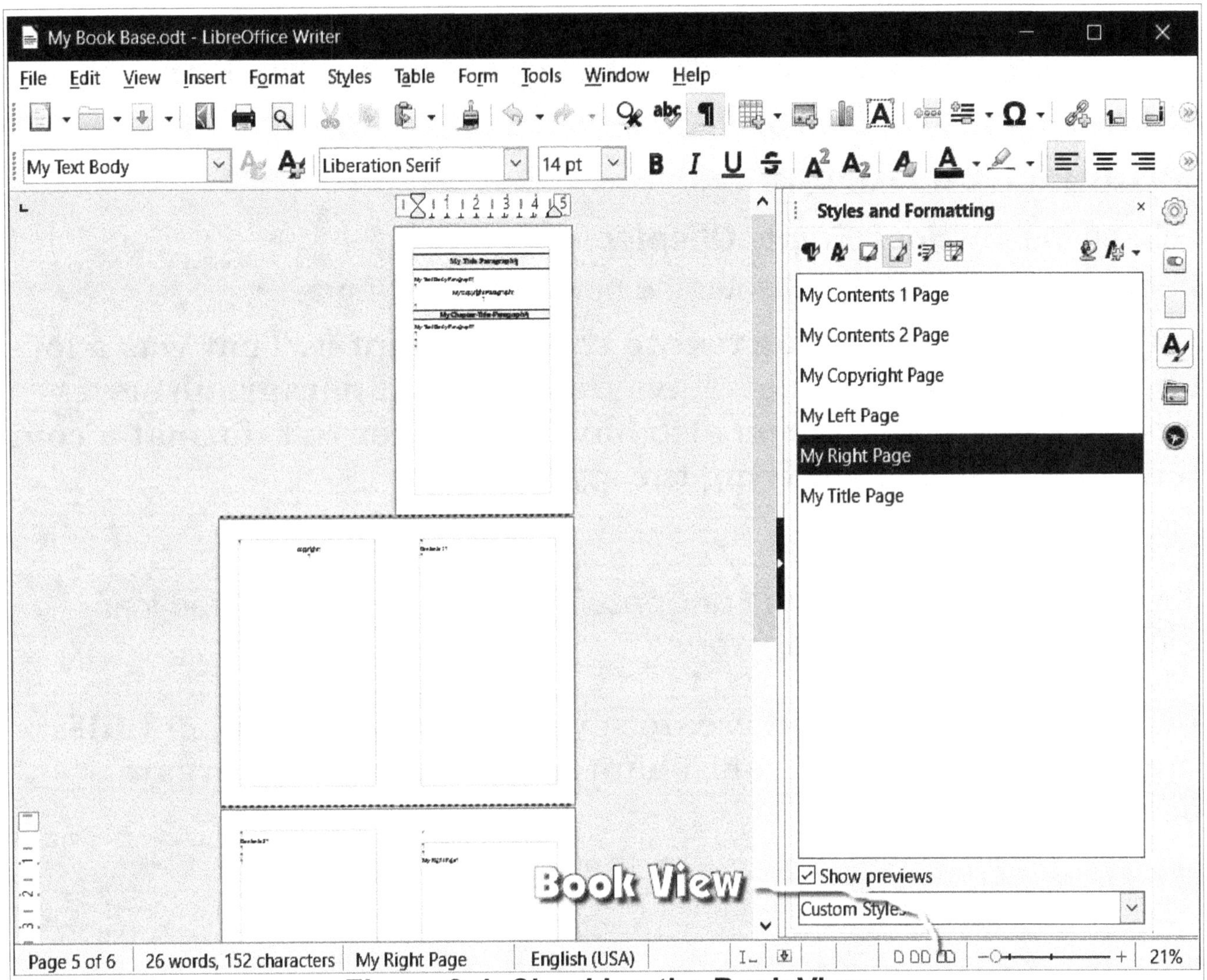

Figure 3-4, Checking the Book View.

OK, now you're ready to write your family history, or the next
great novel, or whatever. In this project, separate files will be created for each chapter. Once the chapters are complete, they will be
copied and pasted into a complete book.

✔ Be sure that you have saved the latest version of the **My Book Base** document.

✔ With the **My Book Base** document open, select *File, Save As* and enter
My Book Empty Chapter as the new file name.

This preserves your *Book Base* file for future use. The *My Book Empty Chapter* will be used each time a new chapter is started.

- ✔ Select the **My Right Page** style.
- ✔ Remove all text from the first page.
- ✔ Enter a title for the chapter and select the **My Chapter Paragraph Style**.
- ✔ Save the *My Book Empty Chapter* document

Starting a New Chapter.

- ✔ Open the *My Book Empty Chapter* file.
- ✔ Select **File, Save As** and enter the new **Chapter Name**.

Now you can start adding text to the new chapter. That was a lot of busy work. But, you now have the page and paragraph styles you need for the book. You also have the power to reformat a complete book just by modifying the styles.

- ✔ Enter text for the chapter.

If you want to create a *Table of Contents* for the book, you need to include *My Heading 1 Paragraphs*.

You should go ahead and create several Chapter document files. When you have created your chapters, return here to create a book document

As an example, I have created a sample book, The Andersson Family. You should substitute your own document files.

- ✔ Open the **My Book Base** document.
- ✔ Select **File, Save As** and enter the location and name of your book.
- ✔ Select **File, Properties**, select the *Description* tab, and enter the **Title** for your book.

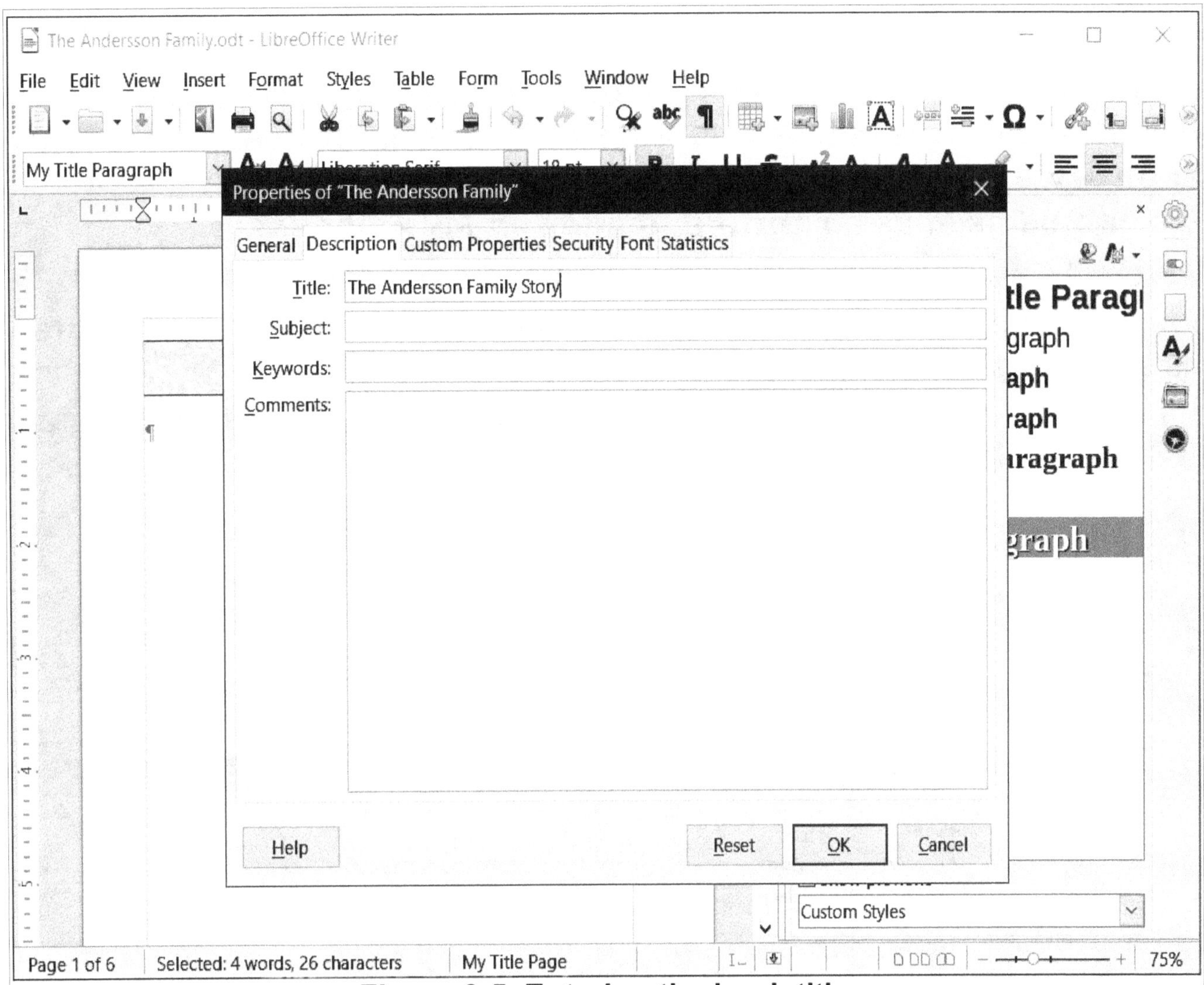

Figure 3-5, Entering the book title.

There are still a few details to attend to. For example the title and chapter headings can be used in headers.

✔ Go to the **Title Page** of the book, highlight the title text, and then **Insert, Field,** and select **Title**.

✔ Go to the first **My Left Page**, and in the **header**, **Insert, Field,** and select **Title**.

The book title will now appear on the header of every My Left Page. You can also insert the book title in the header of My Right Page. Some authors will put their name in the left or right page headers. There are a variety of options for left and right headers.

 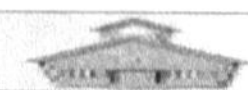

Running Headers

Sometimes you will see a book that has what is called a *running header.* Running headers pick up the most recent designated paragraph style and place it in a header. Here is how the *My Chapter Title* can be used as a running header on *My Right* pages.

✔ From the *Menubar*, select **Tools, Chapter Numbering**.

✔ In the *Chapter Numbering* dialog box, select **My Chapter Title Paragraph** as the *Paragraph style*.

✔ If you are going to include a *Table of Contents*, set the *Level 2* Paragraph style to **My Heading 1 Paragraph**.

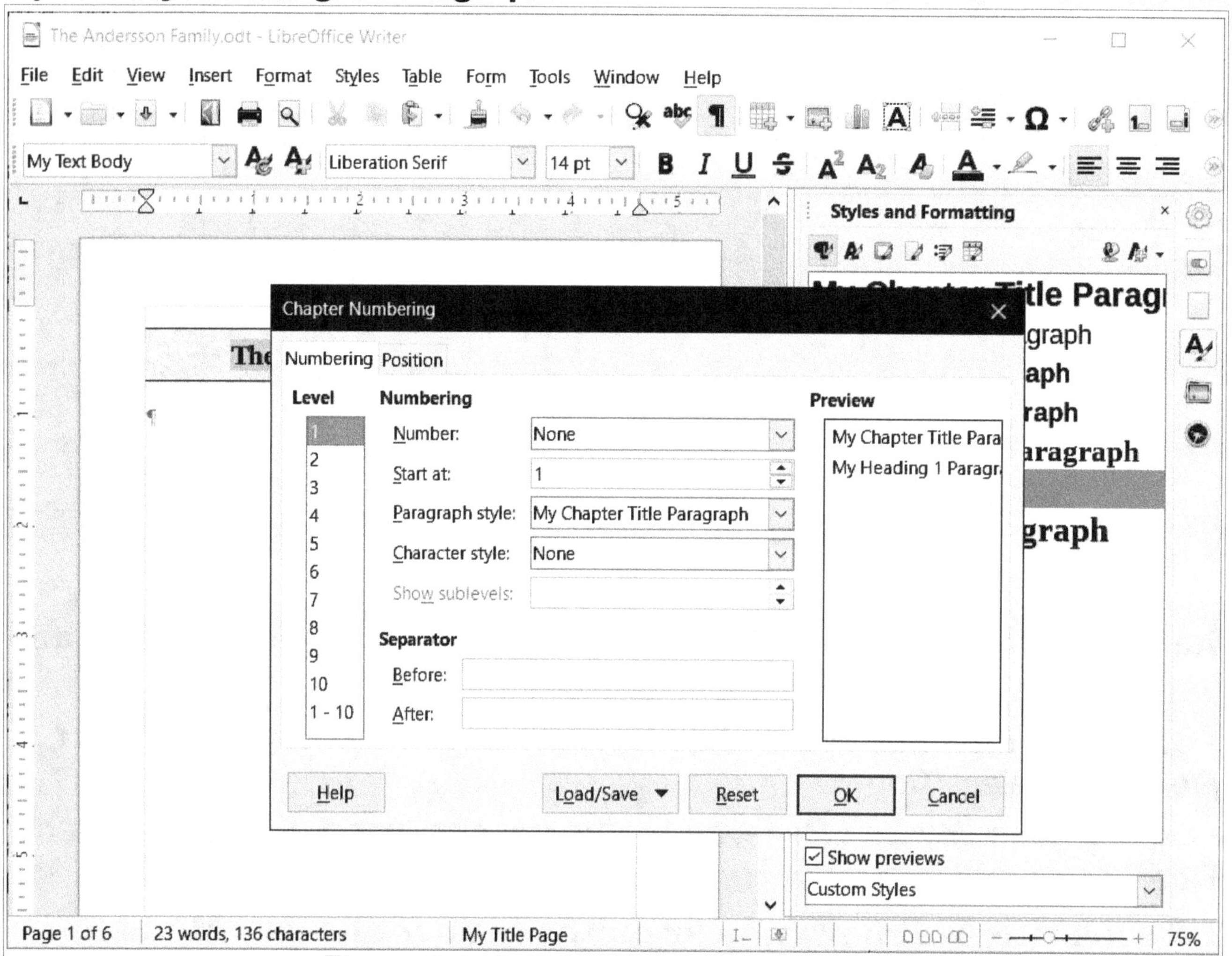

Figure 3-6, Setting Chapter numbering.

✔ Next, place the cursor in a *My Right Page* header.

✔ Select **Insert, Field, Chapter**.

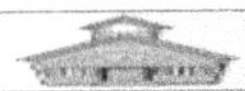

You won't see anything in the **My Right Page Header** until after you have added some chapters to your book. By now, you should know how to create custom paragraph styles for *Headers* and *Footers*. As my lazy professors used to say "I'll leave that as an exercise for the student."

Now it's time to add chapter contents to your book.

- Keep the book document open in a Window.
- **Open** your **Chapter 1** document in a second window. Use **Ctrl+A** to select all of the Chapter 1 material and then **Copy** it to the clipboard.
- Place the text cursor in the first **My Right Page** of your **book document** and **Paste** the contents from Chapter 1.

> Don't forget to save your book file frequently.

- Select **Ctrl+Home** to jump to the last page of the book document.
- If the last page is not empty, select **Ctrl+Enter** to force a page break.

Authors who prefer to have each chapter start on a right facing page can simply use **Ctrl+Enter** to force a new page if the previous chapter ends on an odd page. There are endless ways for authors to create books that go beyond just plain text on each page. However, if you are creating a basic text only novel, you needn't worry about any of these formatting tricks.

Now you should repeat the process of pasting your chapter contents until all chapters have been added to the book.

Once the chapters have been added, a *Table of Contents* can be inserted.

- Place the text cursor in the **Contents 1** page of your book file.
- Select **Insert, Table of Contents, Table of Contents.**

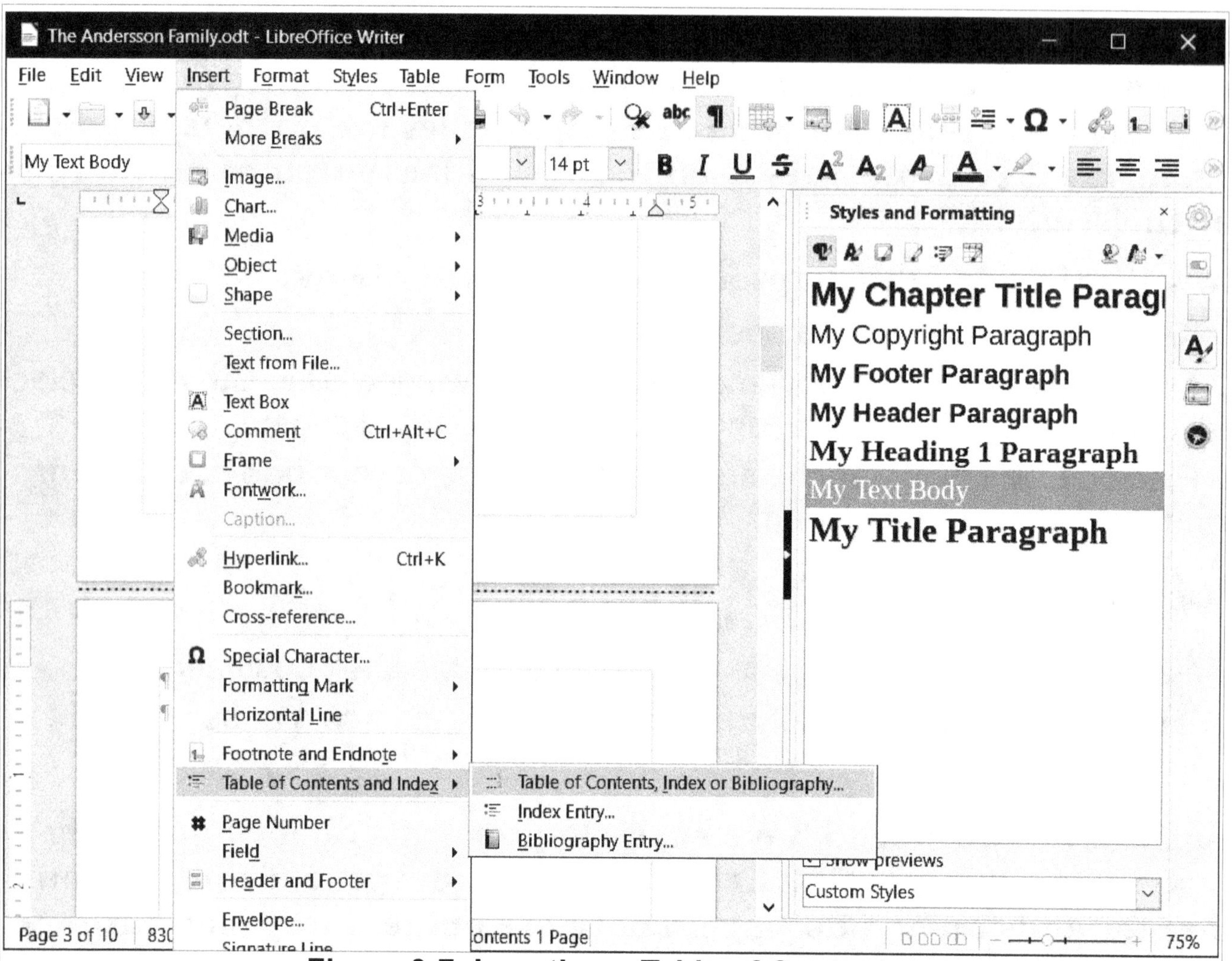

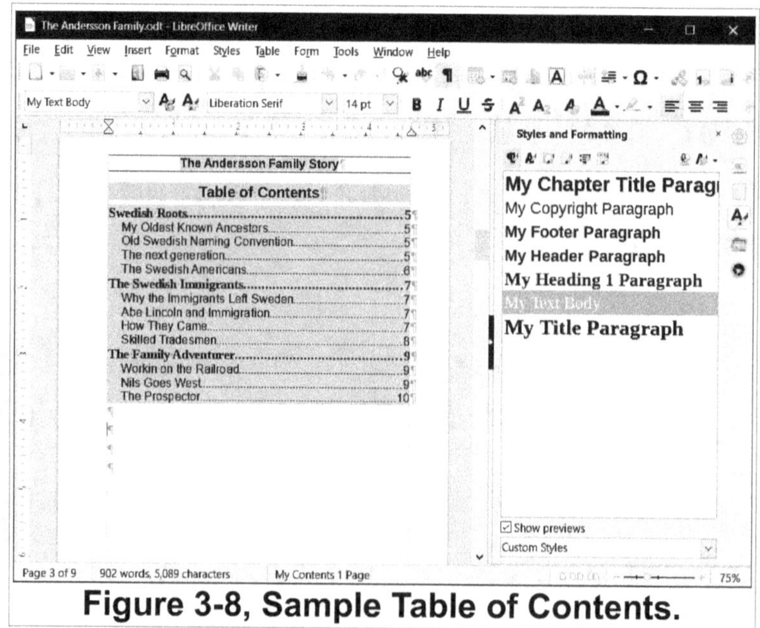

Figure 3-7, Inserting a Table of Contents.

This will add a *Table Of Contents* to your book.

Once again, you have the power to create or modify paragraph styles for the *Table of Contents* entries.

- ✔ If the Table of Contents fits on one page, **Delete** the **Contents 2** page.
- ✔ Insert page numbers in the footers.

Figure 3-8, Sample Table of Contents.

Of course there is still a lot of work to do. A graphic for the *Title Page* can be found or created. Do some enhancing to the *Copyright Page*. You will probably want to add an 'About the Author' section, possibly on the Copyright Page. A lot of novels do not include much in the way of graphics. I suspect that is because most authors are not familiar with tools for dealing with graphic images. However, with LibreOffice Writer, you have the power to incorporate more than just text in your books.

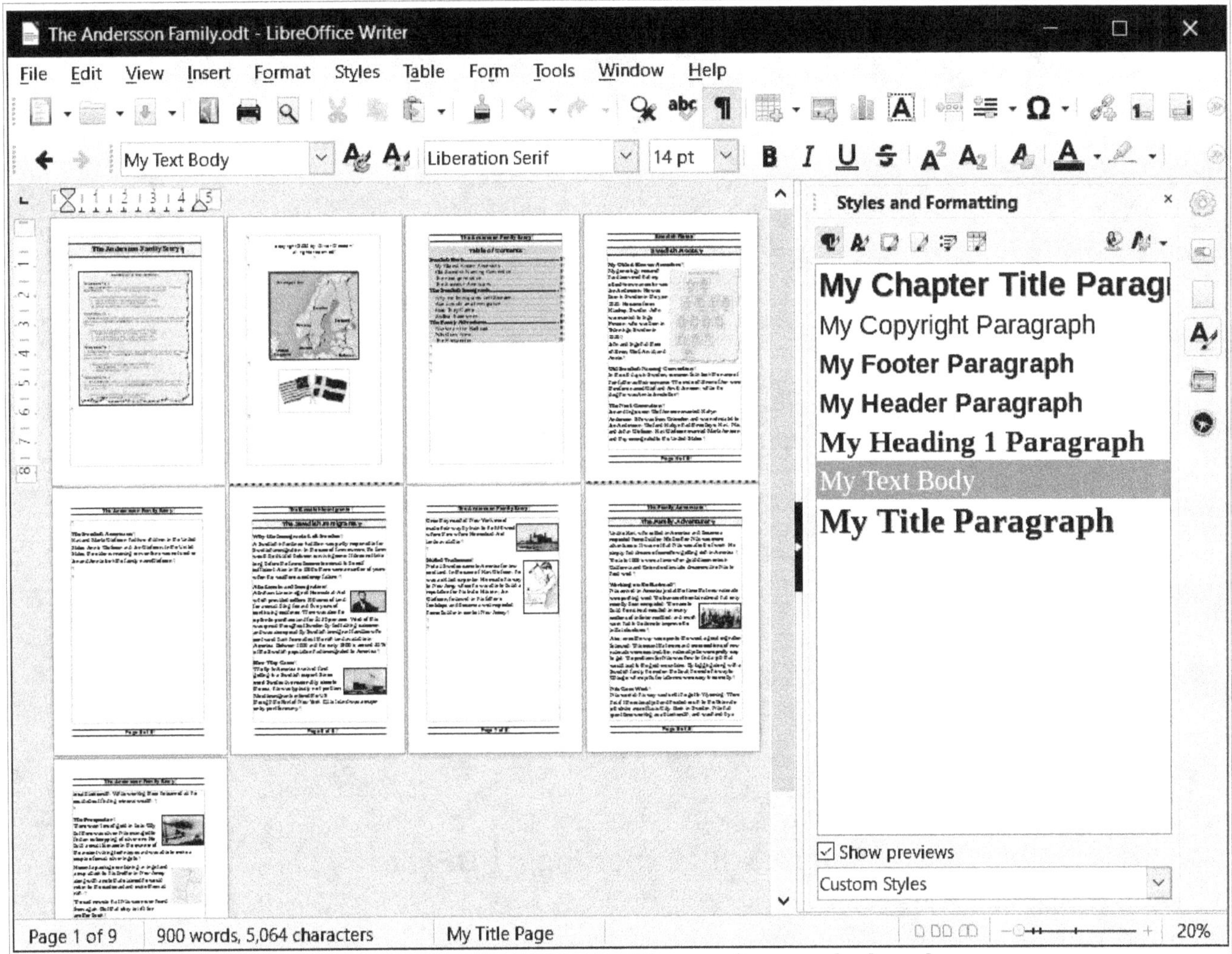

Figure 3-9, Multi Page View of sample book.

Publishing Your Book

There are a few refinements you may want to make, but let's jump ahead and see how to create a file that can be sent to a place like Kindle Direct Publishing.

✓ From the *Menubar*, select **File, Export As, PDF**.

This opens the *PDF Options* dialog box. There are a lot of settings available. If you have any graphics images in your book, be sure to set resolution to at least 300 dpi.

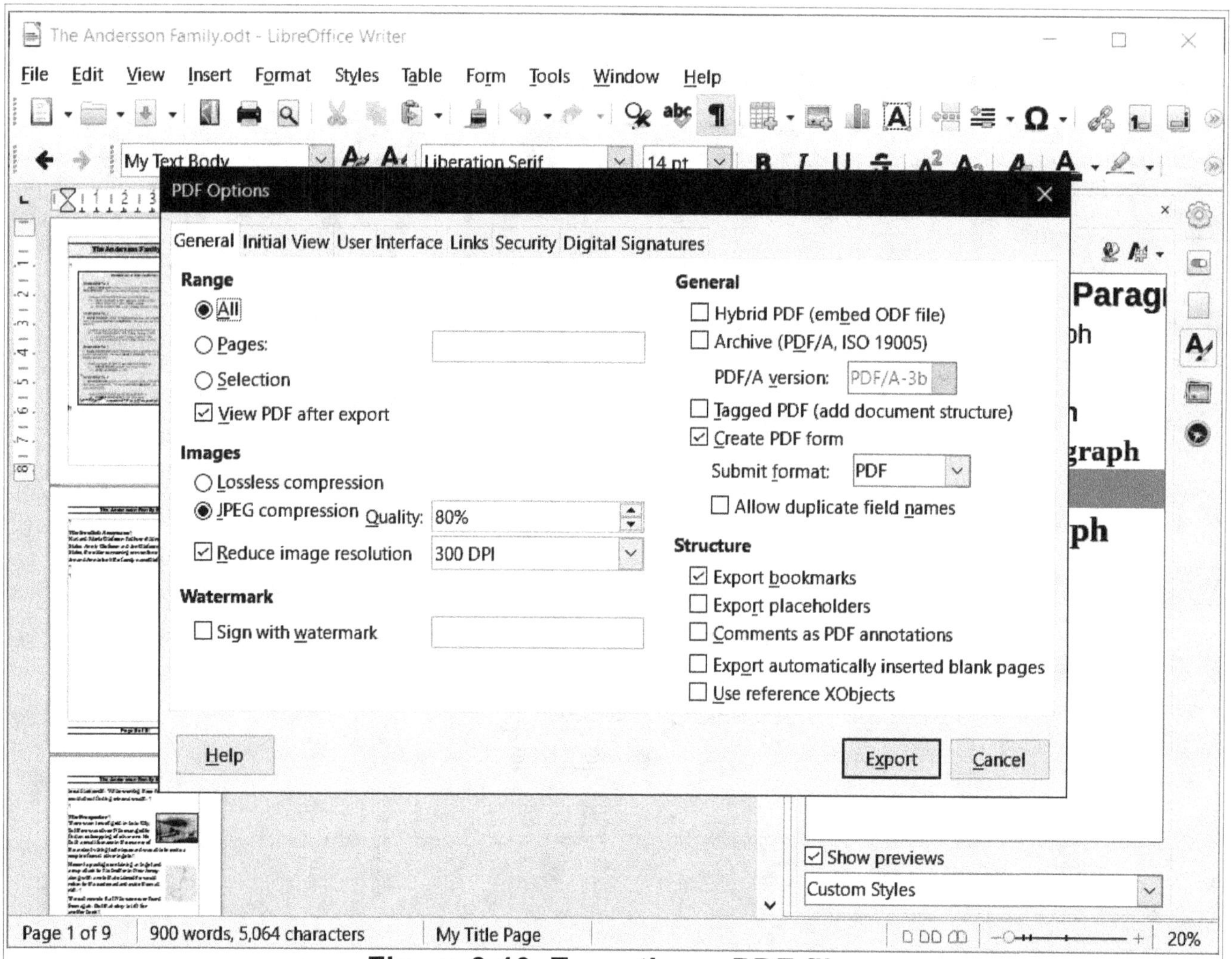

Figure 3-10, Exporting a PDF file.

You can explore the different options tabs, but most only have to do with how to display your PDF file locally. Once you download your file to kdp, you will have additional opportunities to review your book before publishing.

When you have exported your PDF file, you can open it to see how your book will look to your readers. Since most writers are not their own best proof readers, it is a good idea to have the PDF ver-

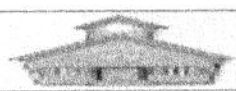

sion reviewed by someone with good editing abilities. If the PDF file is not too large, it can be sent by email. Large files can be copied to a flash drive for review by editors.

Have fun creating your books.

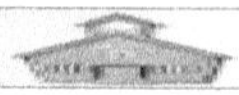

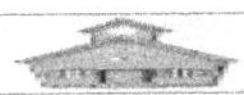

Project 4 ~ Creating A Two Column Newsletter

Introduction

This Project will cover some of the basics for creating a newsletter or similar two column document. Most newsletters have a standard format that is repeated in each issue. This is a natural application for LibreOffice Writer since once the page and paragraph styles have been established, the editor need only worry about content for each new issue.

Creating Styles

- ✓ **Open** a new LibreOffice Writer document.
- ✓ Select *File, Save As*, and enter **My Newsletter** as the file name.
- ✓ From the *Menubar*, select **File, Properties** and enter **My LibreOffice Writer Newsletter** as the *Title*.
- ✓ In the *Sidebar*, select *Styles and Formatting*.
- ✓ In the *Styles and Formatting* Sidebar, select **Custom**.
- ✓ Go through the *Paragraph*, and *Page* styles and delete any entries.
- ✓ Select the *Styles and Formatting* Page option.

Your document should now look similar to Figure 4-1.

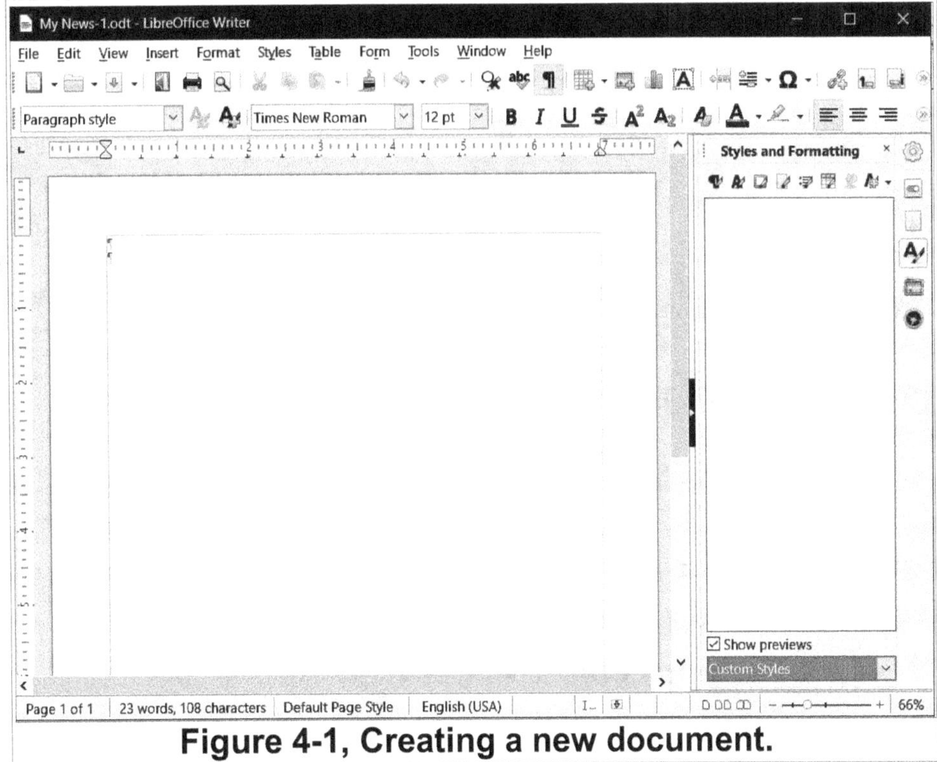

Figure 4-1, Creating a new document.

Our newsletter project will have three *Page Styles*; *My News First*, *My News Left*, and *My News Right*.

✔ *Right click* in the *Page Styles* Sidebar *Custom* area and select **New**.

✔ In the *Organizer* tab, enter the *Name* **My News Left**.

✔ Make *My News Left* be the **Next** page style.

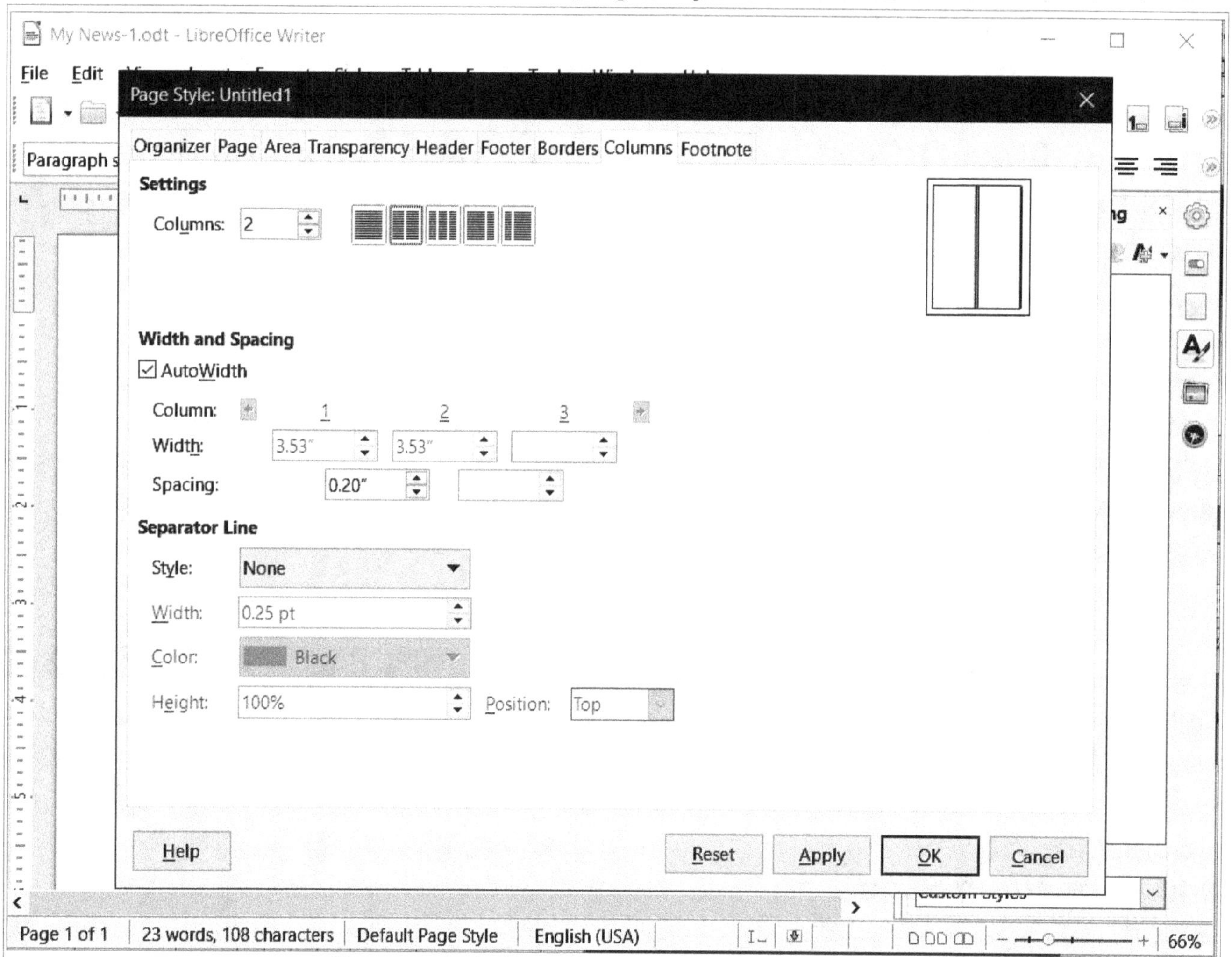

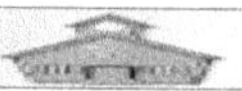

Figure 4-2, Creating a new page style.

This will be changed to *My News Right* later.

✔ In the *Page* tab, enter **0.75** for the *Right Margin*, and **0.50** for the other margins.

Since this is a left page, the right margin needs to be larger for double sided printing.

✔ In the *Columns* tab, set the *Columns* to **2**.

Note that the default spacing between columns is 0.20. If you change this, the column widths will be automatically adjusted.

✓ Toggle the *Headers* and *Footers* **on**.

✓ Select **OK** to complete the page style.

Next, the *My News Right* page style will be created. This is the same as My Left News page, except that the *Next* page style will be My News Left, and the left Margin will be larger.

✓ Create the **My Right News** page.

Next, the *My News First* page style will be created. The settings will be the same as for the My Right News style.

✓ Create the **My News First** page style.

✓ *Right click* on the **My News Left** page style and select **Modify**.

✓ Make the *Next* style be the **My Right News** style.

Now the newsletter page styles are complete. You should check the styles by setting the first page style to *My News First*, and then using **Ctrl+Enter** to force at least 3 pages.

Place the text cursor at the beginning of the first page.

✓ *Double click* on **My First News** page style.

✓ **Enter** some empty paragraphs and use **Ctrl+Enter** to force at least three pages.

✓ Select **Book View** and zoom out to verify the page styles and margins.

Next, the first page will be designed. The *Title* field will be inserted in the first page *Header*. Then a new paragraph style will be created for the newsletter title.

✓ Place the text cursor in the *My News First* page **Header**.

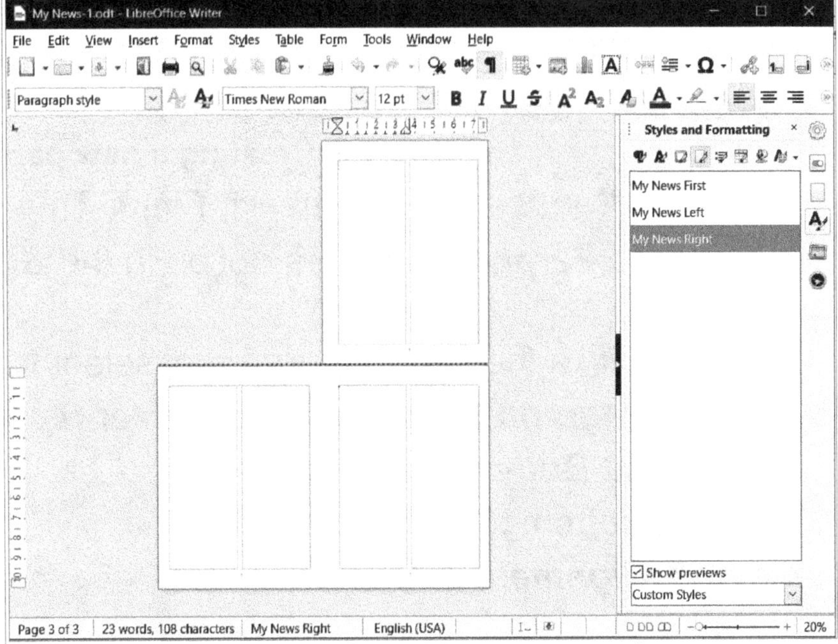
Figure 4-3, Checking page styles.

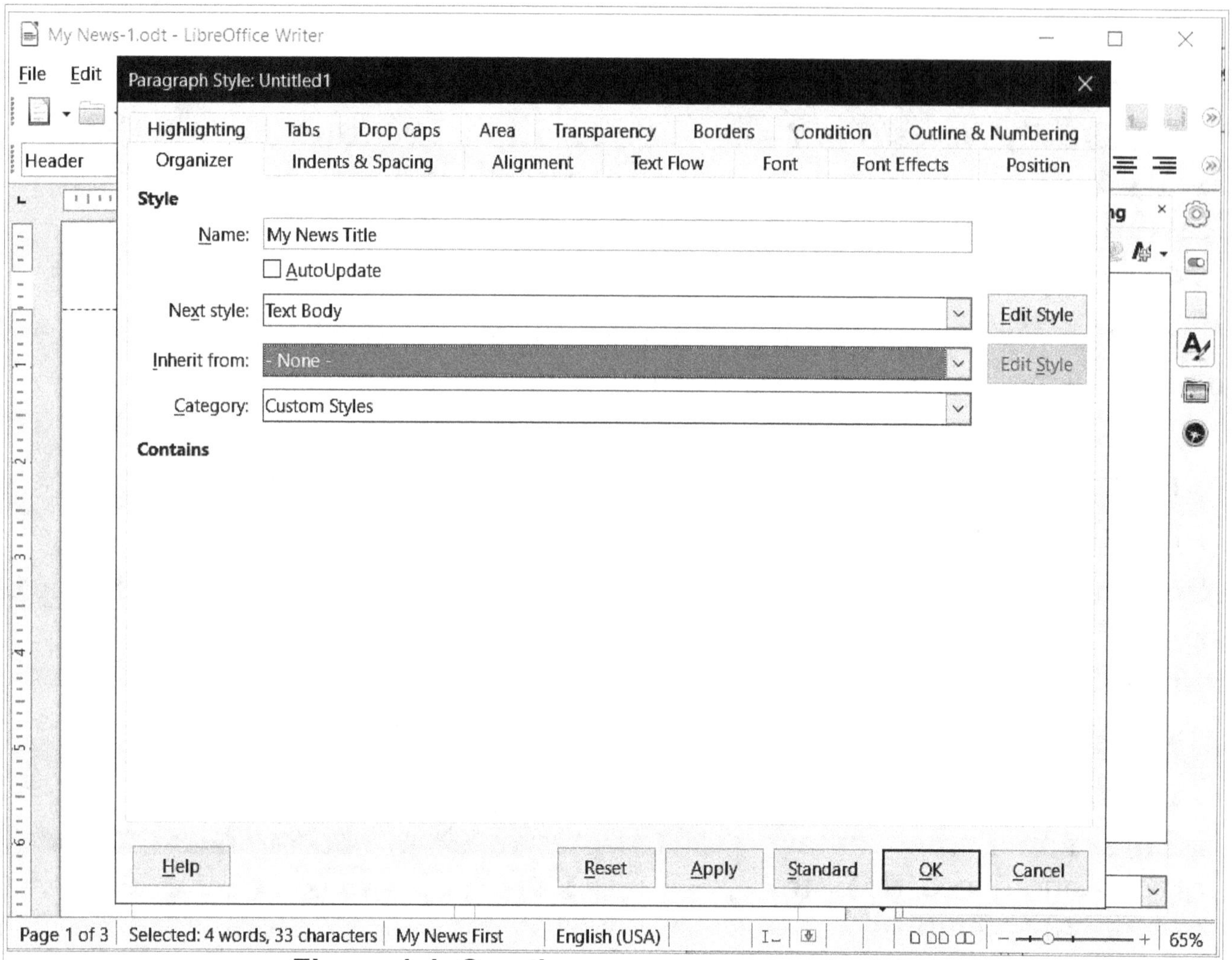

Figure 4-4, Creating a new paragraph style.

✔ From the *Menubar*, select **Insert, Field, Title**.

✔ Select the **Paragraph Styles** option in the *Styles and Formatting* Sidebar.

✔ *Right click* in the *Custom* area and select **New**.

✔ In the *Paragraph Style* dialog box, enter **My News Title** as the *Name*.

✔ Select **Text Body** as the *Next* style.

✔ Set *Inherit* from to **None**.

✔ Set the *Alignment* to **Center**.

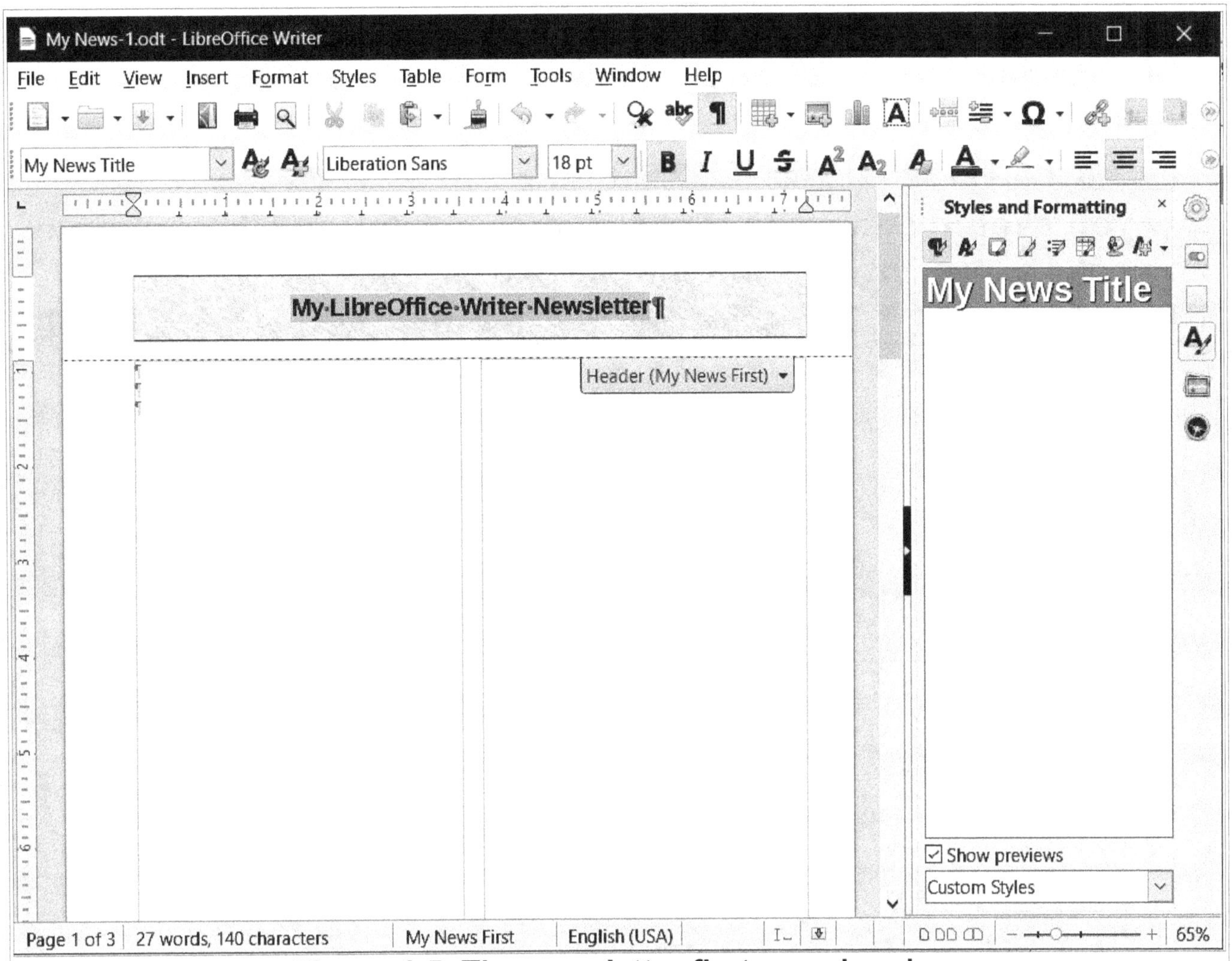

Figure 4-5, The newsletter first page header.

✔ Select your preferred *Font* style. (The sample uses *Liberation Sans, Bold, 18*, and the *Shadow* Font Effect.)

✔ Set the *Border* options. (The example uses *Top* and *Bottom* borders, *Padding Top* and *Bottom* **0.20**.)

✔ Set the *Area* fill as desired. (The example uses *Bitmap, Marble*.)

Observe that the *Header* extends across the page above the columns. This is an opportunity to be creative. You can insert additional paragraphs, images, and even Frames in the first page header. In this example, a date field will be added to the first page header.

Inserting a Date Field

✔ Place the text cursor at the end of the title paragraph and press the **Enter** key.

- From the *Insert TAB*, select **Insert, Field, Date**.
- *Double click* on the date and in the *Edit Fields* dialog box, select your preferred date format.
- Set the **Paragraph Style** for the date to **My News Title**.

Now you should add some text to your newsletter. The example shows the *Lorem ipsum* placeholder text.

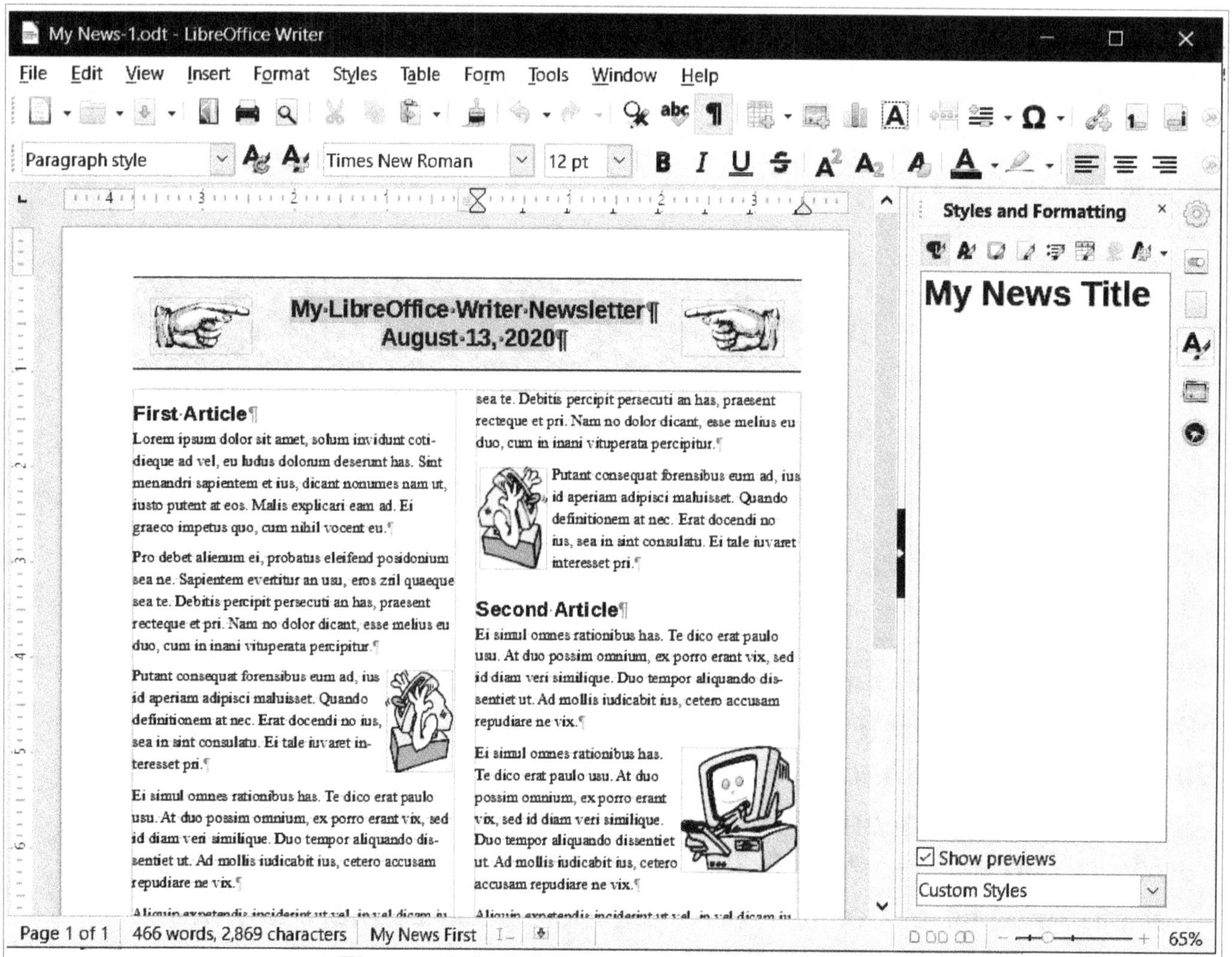

Figure 4-6, Adding text and graphics.

Have you saved your document lately?

If you have completed Projects 1 and 2, you should have enough information to add your own text, create custom paragraph styles, insert graphic images, and more.

When you have created a basic newsletter document, you can use *File, Save As* to preserve it with a new file name. Each time you want to create a newsletter with the same formatting, *Open* your

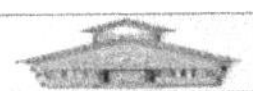

basic newsletter file, do *File, Save As* to create a new edition. Then all you have to do is replace the contents. The busy work that went into formatting the first newsletter does not have to be repeated. This is one of the most powerful features of Word Processing.

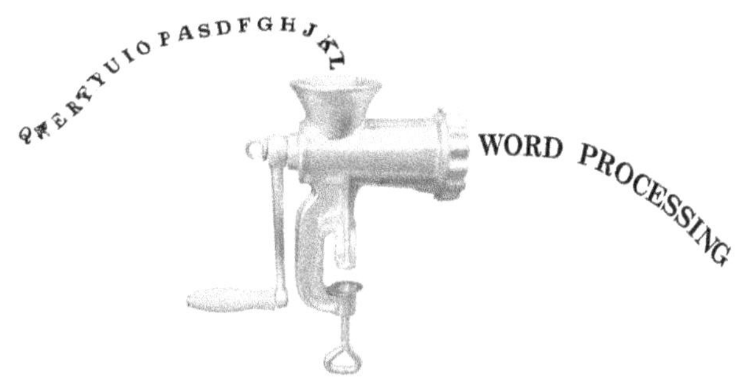

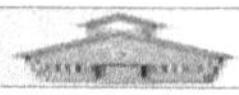

Project 5 ~ Creating Greeting Cards

Introduction

If you want to create your own greeting cards, but you do not want to spend money on special software, or be limited by commercial greeting card software formats, you are in luck. It turns out that with just a little effort you can use LibreOffice Writer to create custom greeting cards.

The following instructions are for creating a four page greeting card by folding an 8 ½ by 11 sheet of paper in half twice. Most office supply stores in the USA carry envelopes that are designed to fit this size card. Look for envelopes that are 4 3/8 by 5 3/4 inches. (If you are outside the USA, adjust measurements as required.)

Plan Ahead

The first step is to determine the relative orientation of the four pages of your greeting card. (This example uses a *Portrait* layout card. *Landscape* layout could also be used.) Take a piece of paper and fold it twice. For the vertical portrait format book fold card in this project, the sheet must be folded in half twice as shown.

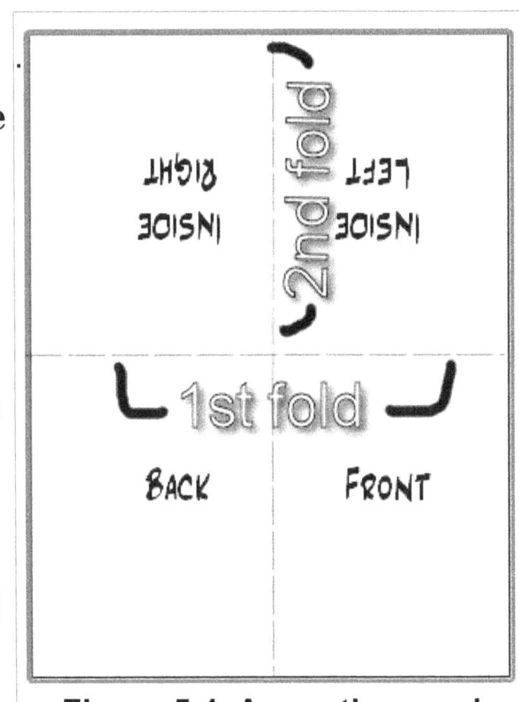

Figure 5-1, A greeting card layout page.

✔ First, fold the sheet in half along a horizontal line (with the sheet in portrait mode).; then fold the sheet a second time.

✔ When you have folded the sheet, write the names of the four pages of the final card on each page and unfold it (see Figure 5-1).

When you unfold the sheet you will see how the four pages have to be arranged.

✔ Open a new LibreOffice Writer document.

✔ Select **File, Save As**, adjust the **Save As** folder as required, and enter a file **Name** for your greeting card.

The LibreOffice Writer display is shown in Figure 5-2.

Figure 5-2, New greeting card document.

✔ If the **Sidebar** is not shown, from the **Menubar** select **View, Sidebar**.

✔ In the **Sidebar**, select the **Styles** option.

✔ If there are any Custom Paragraph or Page Styles shown in the Custom list, delete them.

✔ If the **Drawing Toolbar** is not shown, from the **Menubar** select **View, Toolbars, Drawing**.

We will create a custom **Page Style** for our cards.

✔ In the **Sidebar Styles and Formatting** option, select the **Page Styles** option.

✔ With the **Custom** list on the display, right click in the styles list and select **New**.

- ✓ In the *Page Style* dialog box *Organizer TAB*, enter **My Card Page** for the *Name* and *Next style*.
- ✓ In the *Page TAB*, enter **0.50** for all four margins.
- ✓ Make sure *Headers* and *Footers* are **OFF**. Then, select **OK** to close the dialog box.

Setting the card page margins to **0.5** will make it easier to calculate precise locations for the different objects placed in the front and back areas of the card.

Creating A Card Layout

Making the four sections of the card fit the page nicely after it is printed and folded is a bit tricky. In the next section, we will create a card layout document with rectangles that can be used as guides to properly locate objects on the different parts of the card. These rectangles can easily be deleted when the card design is finished.

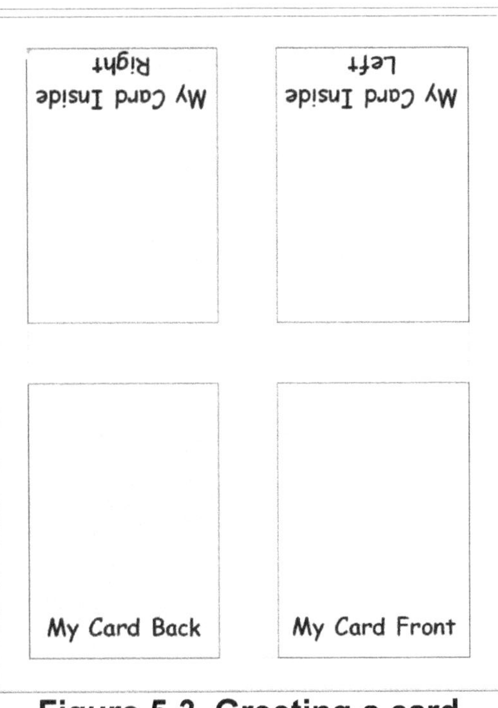

Figure 5-3, Greeting a card layout.

> *Drag* a drawing object means click at the a corner of the object, hold the left mouse button down and drag the mouse cursor to the opposite corner of the object. The Drag function works the same on any Drawing object.

- ✓ From the *Drawing Tool Bar,* select the **Rectangle** tool.
- ✓ Drag a rectangle from the upper left margin down and to the right a couple of inches.

Don't worry about the size. We will set it precisely in the next step.

- ✓ *Right click* on the rectangle and select the **Position and Size** option from the context menu.
- ✓ In the *Position and Size* dialog box, enter a width of **3.25**, and a *Height* of **4.5**.
- ✓ Set the *Anchor* to **To Page**.

✔ Set the *Horizontal* and *Vertical* positions to **0.50** from the left and top of the page; then select **OK** to close the dialog box.

✔ In the *Sidebar*, Select the *Properties* option, then adjust the *Transparency* to **90%**.

Increasing the Transparency will save printer ink or toner. Now we need three more rectangle. The copy and paste trick will help.

✔ *Right click* on the *rectangle*, then select **Copy**.

✔ Click away from the rectangle, *right click*, and select **Paste**.

You should memorize the shortcut for Copy [**Ctrl+C**] and Paste [**Ctrl+V**].

The copy of the rectangle will be superimposed on the original. You can right click on the copy, select the position and size option, and adjust the position of the copy.

✔ *Right click* on the new rectangle, select the **Position and Size** option from the context menu, and adjust the *Horizontal* position to be **4.75** from the left.

✔ Repeat the Copy and Paste trick two more times. The Vertical position of the lower two rectangles should be **6.0** from the top.

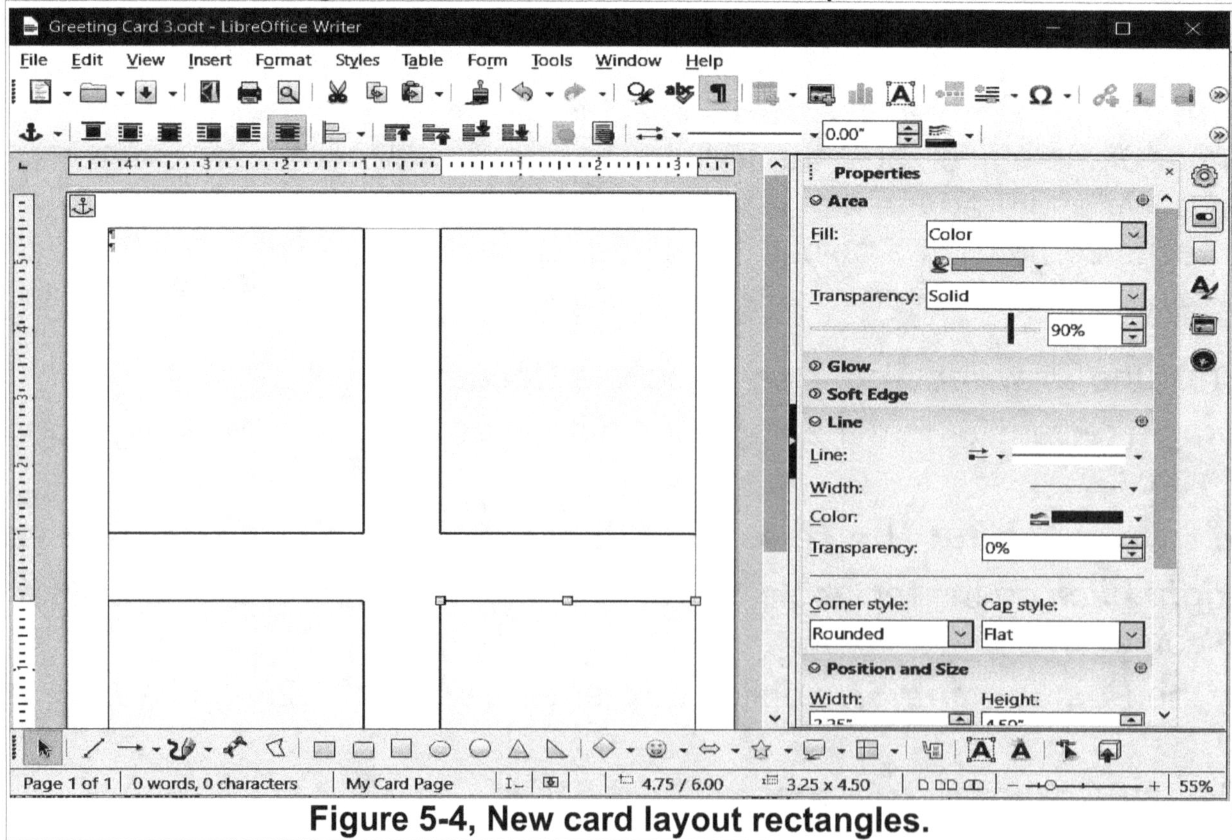

Figure 5-4, New card layout rectangles.

Adding Text:

Next, you will see how to add text to your card.

✓ From the **Drawing Tool Bar,** select the **Text Box** tool.

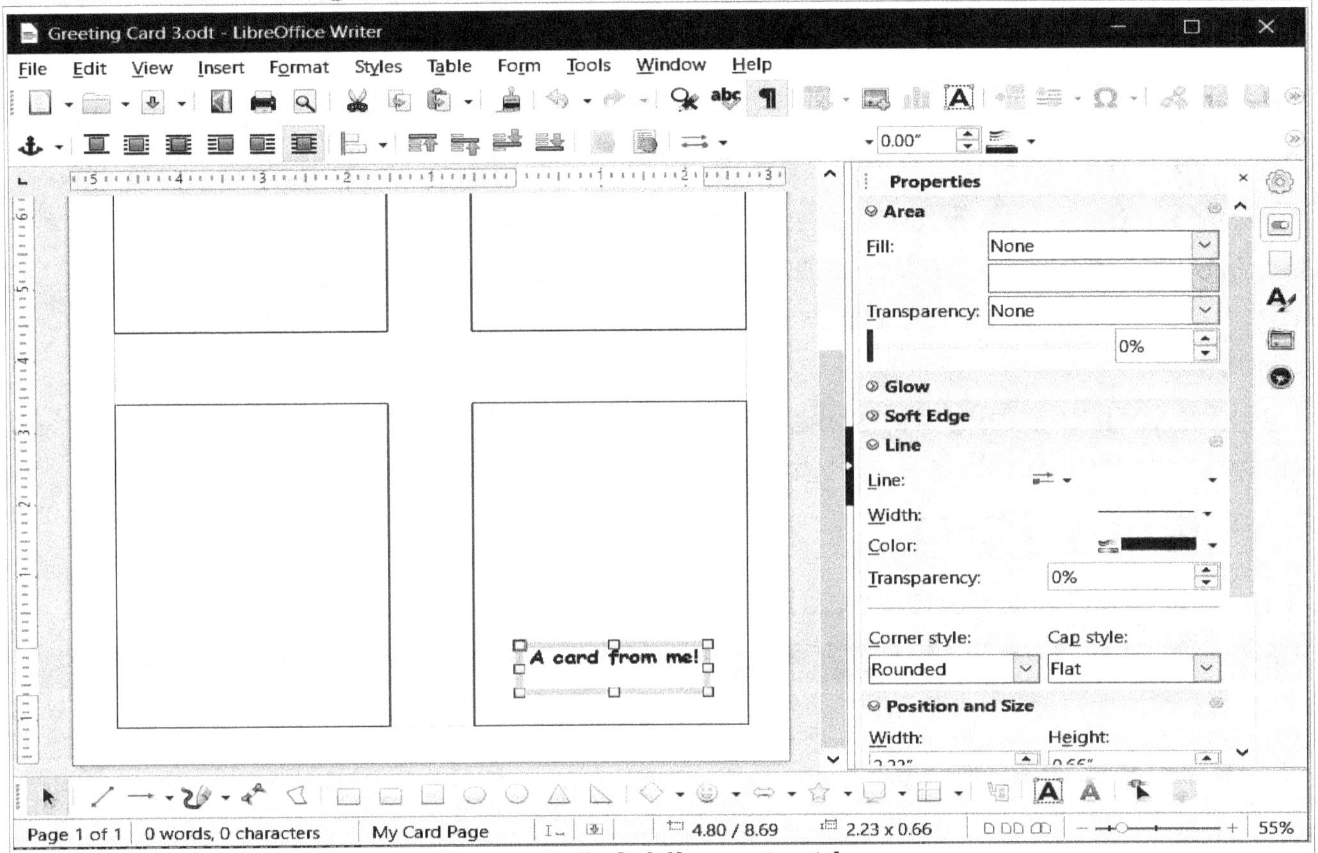

Figure 5-5, Adding a text box.

✓ In the **lower right** quadrant of the page, drag a text box and enter A card from me! in the text box. (Feel free to substitute your own name or text).

After entering your text, select a point outside the text box to deselect it. Click on a point in the text to select the text box. When the text box is selected, there will be an outline of the box that has grab points at the corners and mid points of the box.

When a text box is selected, you can **double click** to place the text cursor in the box for editing.

> **Here are some text editing selection tricks.**
>
> **Single click** to select the text box.
>
> **Double click** on the text to place the text cursor in the text.

Use the **_Backspace, Delete_**, and **_cursor control arrows_** to edit the text.

Double click to select a **_word_**.

Triple click to select **_a line of text_**.

Press **_Ctrl+A_** to select all text.

When text is selected, text formatting options will appear in the **_Toolbar_** and in the **_Properties Sidebar_** (see Figure 5-5). The **_Toolbar_** and the **_Properties Sidebar_** are **_context sensitive._** This means that they automatically change depending on what kind of object is selected.

✓ Select your text and then use the **_Toolbar_** or **_Properties Sidebar_** to adjust the text characteristics.

Moving Text Objects

To move a text object you first have to select the text object.

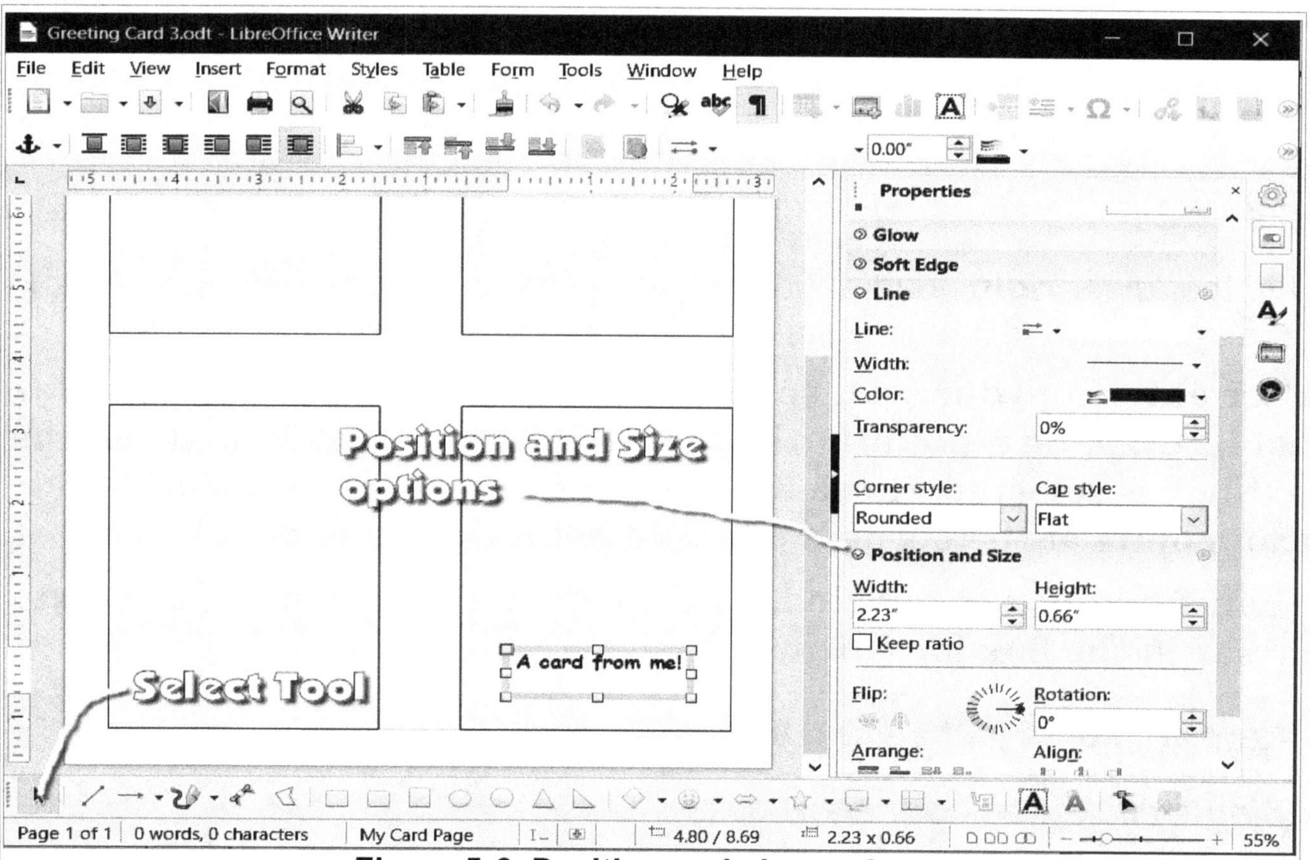

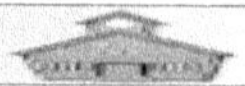

Figure 5-6, Position and size options.

✓ From the **_Drawing Toolbar_**, pick the **Select** tool; then select the text.

When the text box is selected, a boundary line will appear around the text object. This boundary has grab points for changing the size of the text object (but not the font size). If you hover the mouse pointer on the boundary, but not on a grab point, the mouse pointer will change to a double arrow. When the double arrow appears, you can drag the text object to a new location. When a text object is selected, the *Sidebar* provides options for positioning the text object.

Now that you know how to manipulate text, it is time to add and rotate text for the inside right card page.

Rotating Objects

Next, some text will be added to the inside right card page. After the text is added, it will be rotated so that it will be properly oriented after the sheet is folded.

- Select the *Text Box* tool.
- Drag a text box in the *upper left* section of the sheet. (This will end up in the inside right page of the card after it has been folded. See Figure 5-1.)
- Enter the following text pressing the *Enter* key at the end of each line. (Or, enter your own preferred text.)

> Although this text is inside of the card
> The proper placement is very hard.
> And if I miss the center exact,
> I will never escape a critic's attack.

- Format the text as desired.
- With the text box selected, use the *Rotation* option in the *Position and Size Sidebar* and enter a Rotation angle of **180**.

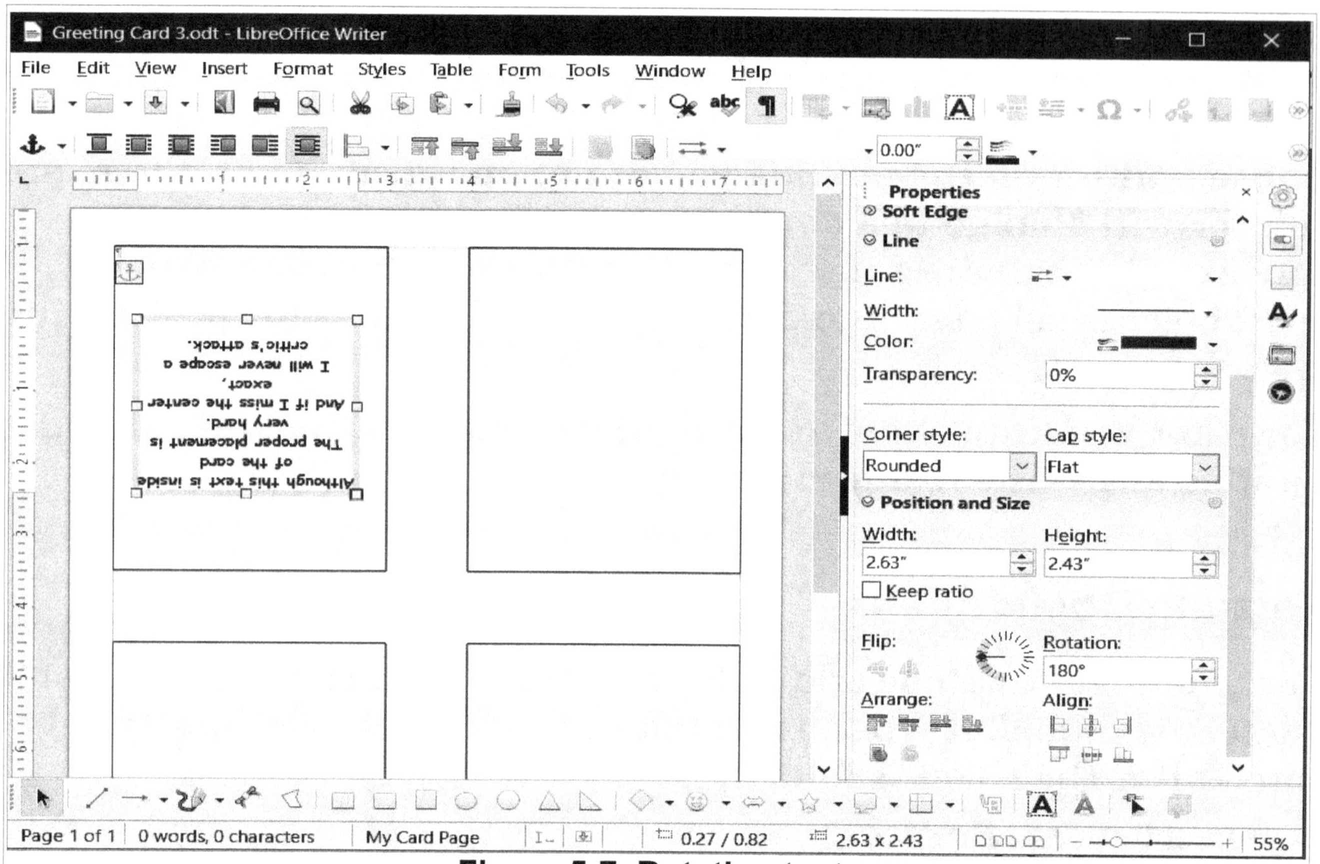

Figure 5-7, Rotating text.

Your text for the inside right card page should now have the proper orientation. However, the default font and style might not be as classy as you might like. You can use the *Toolbar* or *Sidebar* to adjust the text characteristics. Just remember that the Sidebar *Properties options* control only text that is currently *selected*.

Adding a Symbol Shape

Next, we will add a graphic for the back of the card.

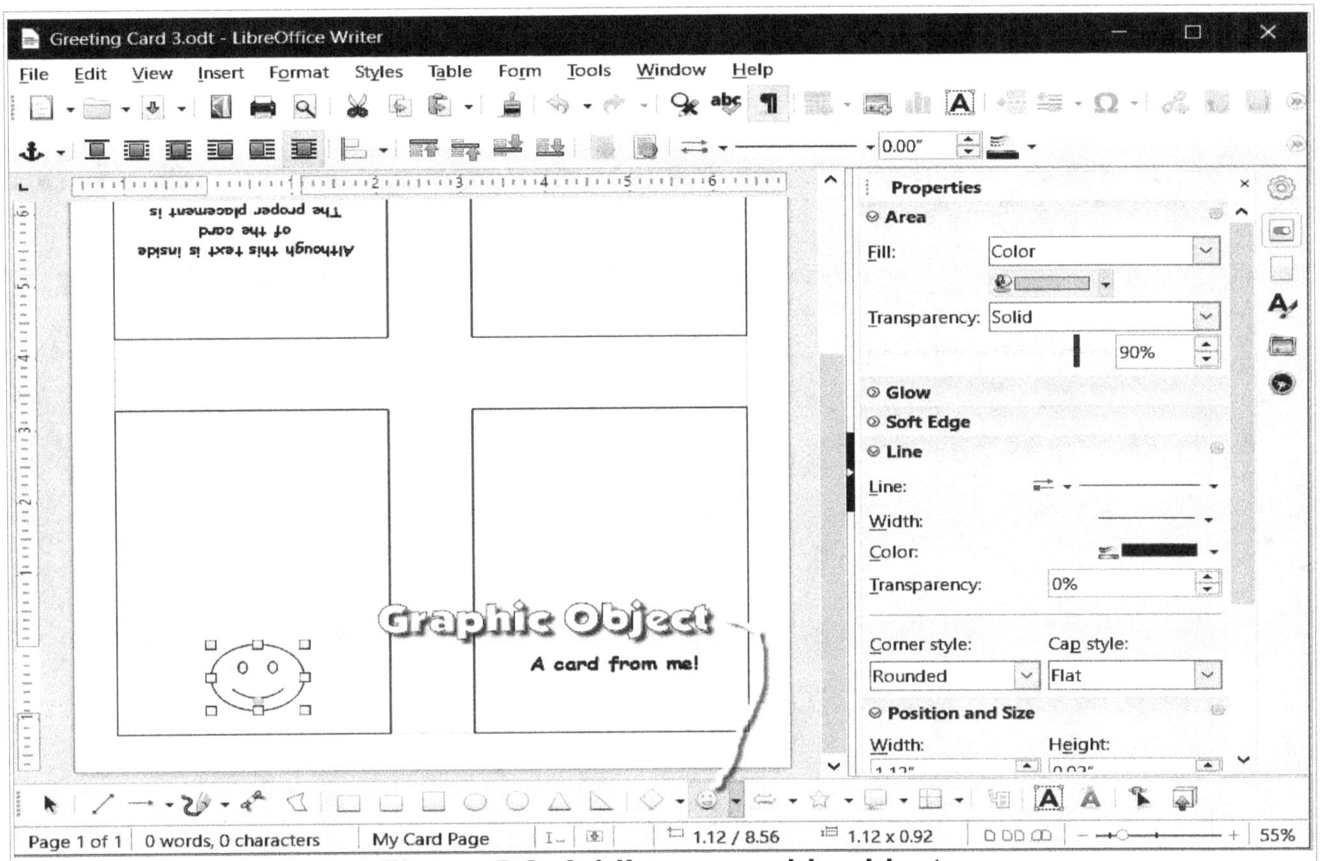

Figure 5-8, Adding a graphic object.

✔ From the ***Drawing Tool Bar***, select the smiley face from the **Symbol Shapes** tool (see Figure 5-8).

✔ Drag out a symbol in the lower left quadrant of the page (this will end up on the back of the card).

Observe that when a graphic object is selected little grab points will be shown at the corners and mid points of the object. You can click and drag these points and change the size of the object.

NOTE: To preserve the aspect ratio of an object that you are resizing, hold the ***shift key down*** while you grab and drag a corner point.

When you move the mouse cursor over a selected graphic object the cursor will change to crossed arrows. With the crossed arrows cursor you can ***drag*** the object to a new position.

✔ Move the happy face to the lower center of the back of the card section.

✔ With the happy face symbol selected, use either the ***Toolbar*** or ***Sidebar Properties*** options to select a new **color** for the happy face and the happy face line.

Adding Pictures:

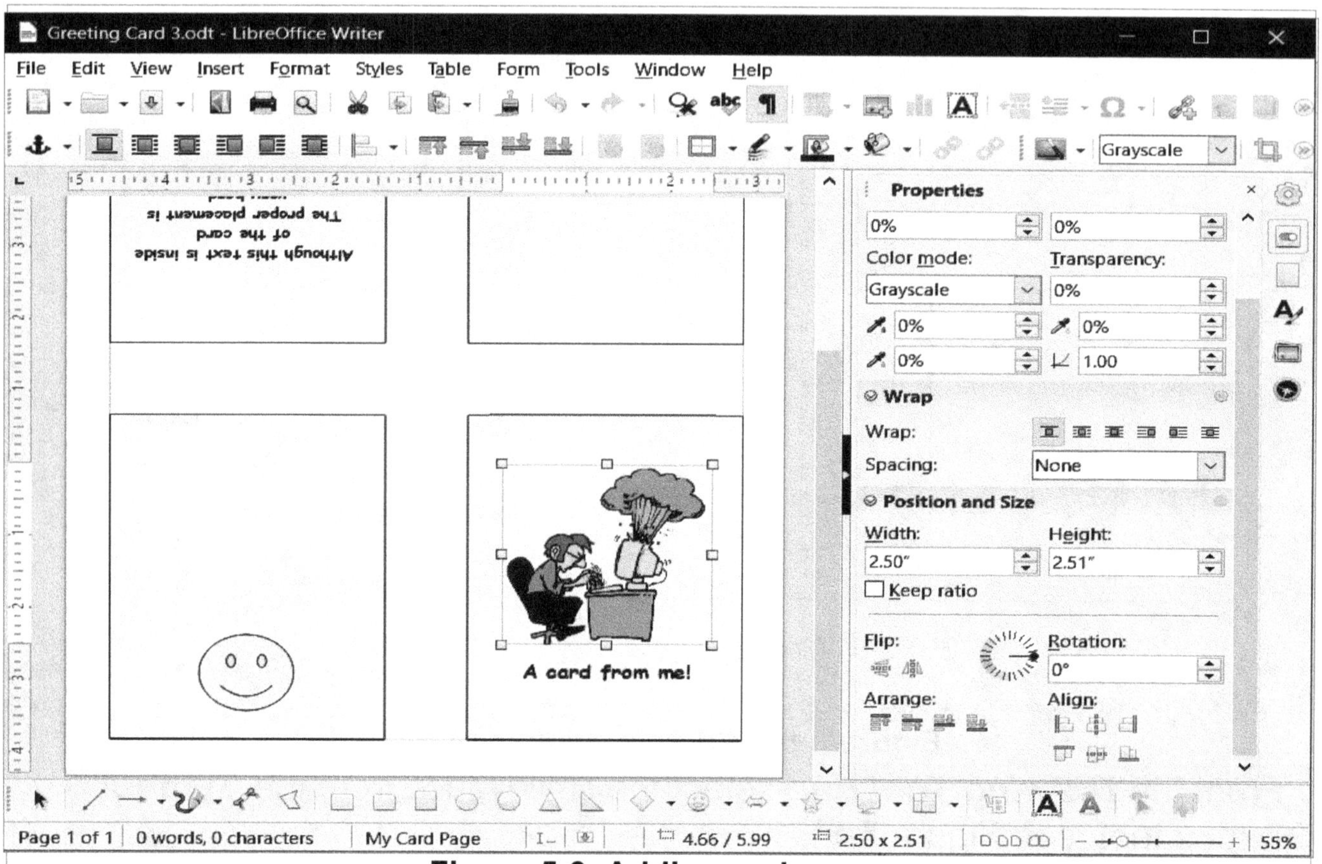

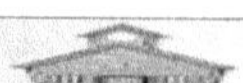

Figure 5-9, Adding an image.

Next, a graphic image will be added to the front page of the card. This is located in the lower right corner of the full sheet.

✔ Make sure that no object is selected (use the Select tool and click in an empty area).

✔ Select **Insert Image**, then use the **Insert Image** dialog box to select a picture of your choice.

Figure 5-9 shows that a graphic image has been inserted and moved to the lower right area of the sheet.

When the image is selected, you can drag the image to the desired location. You can also use the grab points to resize the image. The *Position and Size* options from the *Sidebar* also provide options for adjusting image properties.

✔ Adjust the size and location of your image as desired.

To change the aspect ratio while using a corner grab point to resize the graphic, hold the Shift key down while dragging the grab point.

✔ Select your picture and then **_double click_** on it to open the **_Image_** dialog box.

✔ Review the options of each TAB in the Image dialog box.

Let's add an image to the inside left panel of the card.

✔ Click away from any object to make sure that nothing is selected.

If an object is selected when you insert a new image, the new image will replace the selected object.

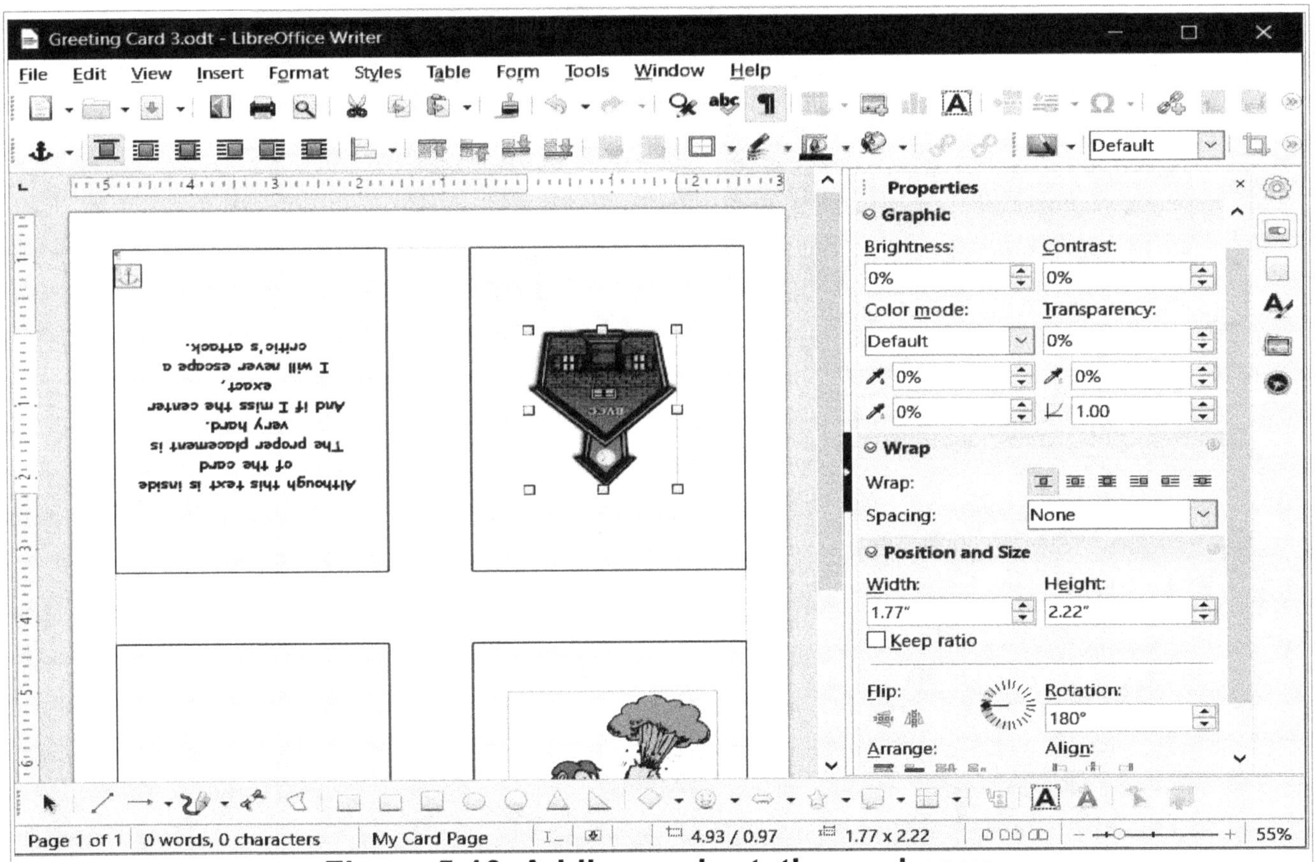

Figure 5-10, Adding and rotating an image.

✔ Select the **Insert Image** tool from the **_TAB Bar_**, then use the **Insert Image** dialog box to select a picture of your choice.

✔ Resize the image and drag it to the left inside panel of the card.

✔ Select the new image and use the **_Sidebar_** to rotate the image 180 degrees.

✔ Add to, or edit your card as desired.

✓ Select *File, Save As* and enter a new file name.

The four colored panels were created to help position objects on the four pages of the card. To remove these panels, select a panel and press the *Delete* key on your keyboard.

Don't forget the *Undo* option.

You now have enough information to create your own custom greeting cards. And, with LibreOffice, it doesn't cost a thing!

✓ Start a *new* document file and go through the steps in this lesson again. This time, use your own words, pictures, and styles.

 **Project 6 ~ Using Tables and Frames in Documents** 

Introduction

Tables are very useful when you want to align sections of text horizontally and vertically. On an old typewriter this was done using tabs and spaces. The problem is that if you use spaces and tabs to align things in word processing, and then change the font size or style, everything will have to be realigned. A table takes all the work out of the alignment process. *Tables* in LibreOffice Writer have many features similar to spreadsheet programs.

Tables or Columns?

Some beginners make the mistake of trying to use page columns to imitate tables. The problem with this is that they have to keep messing with adding and deleting empty paragraphs to keep things aligned between adjacent columns. Columns are designed for newspaper style documents to have the text flow from one column to another. The use of columns can improve reading speeds for many people since the eyes can track faster vertically rather than having to track both horizontally and vertically. However, columns should never be substituted for tables.

Adding Tables:

- Open a new *LibreOffice Writer* document.
- Select *File, Save As* And enter **Table Practice** as the file name.
- Place the text cursor in the second empty paragraph in the document.
- From the *Menubar* select **Table, Insert Table**.
- In the *Insert Table* dialog box enter **Table1** as the *Name*.

✔ Enter **2 columns** and **3 Rows**.

✔ Toggle the *Heading* option **ON**,

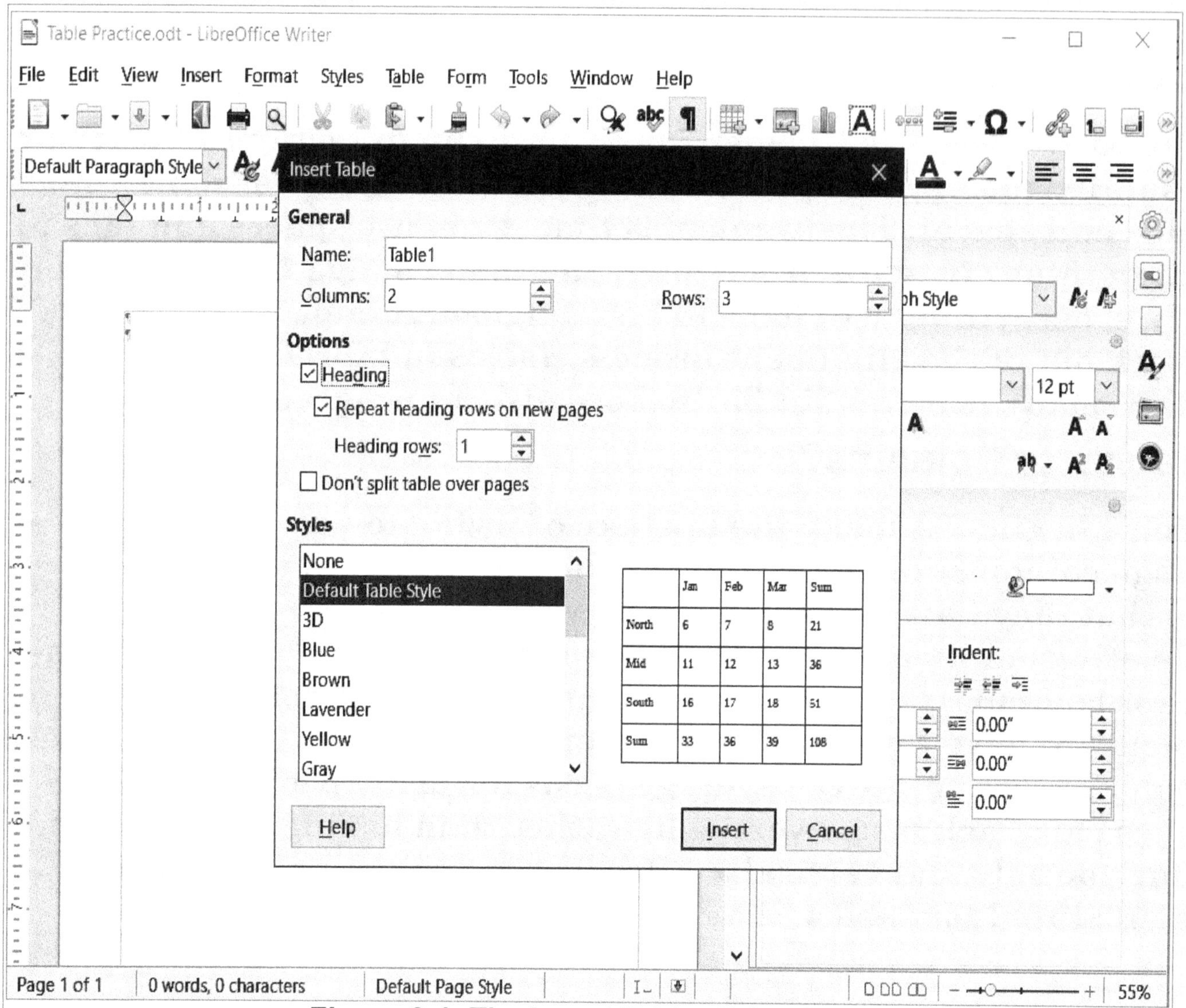

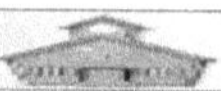

Figure 6-1, The Insert Table dialog box.

✔ Select the **Default Table Style**, then select **Insert**.

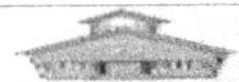

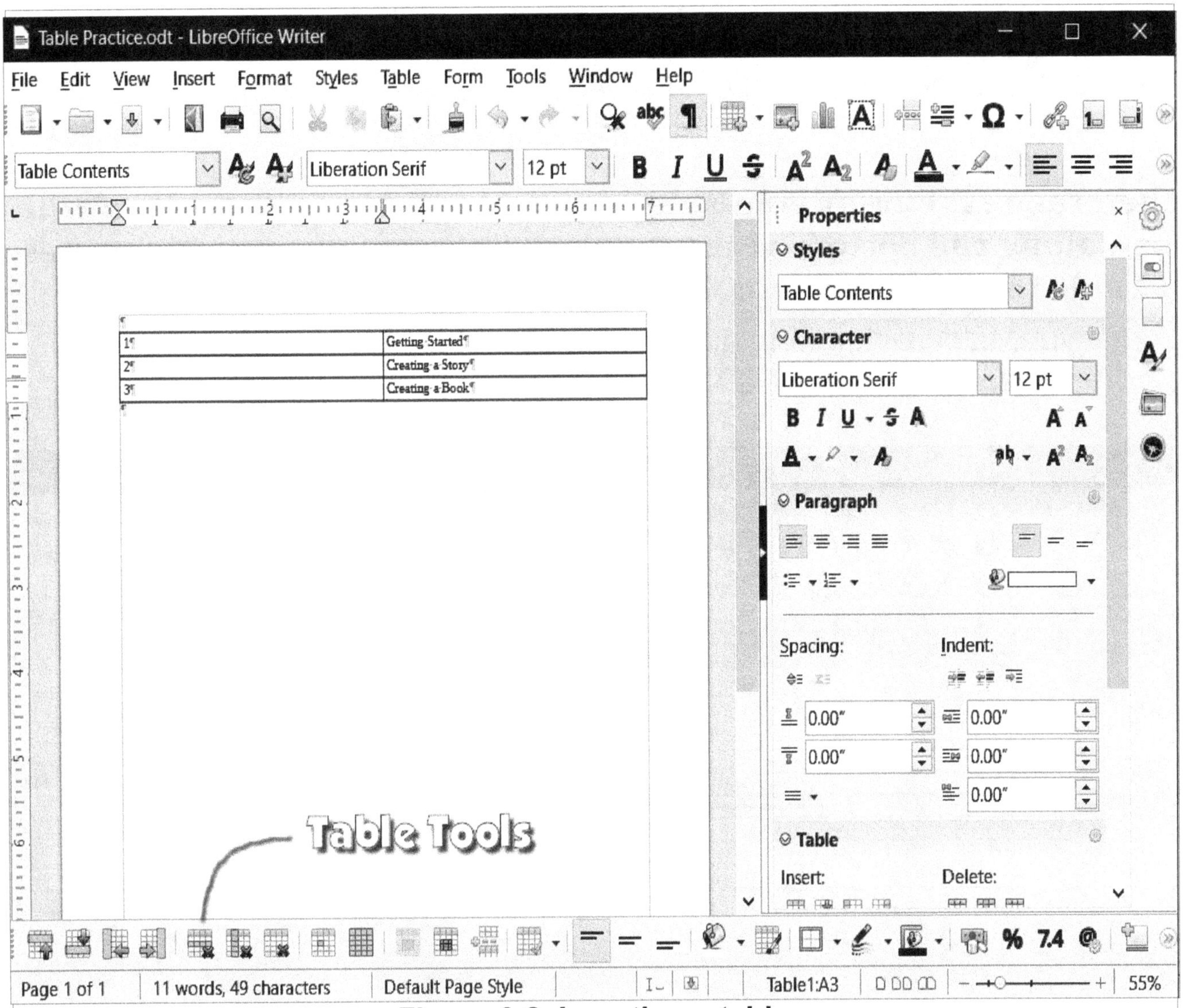

Figure 6-2, Inserting a table.

After entering some text, your table will look similar to Figure 6-2.

There are several points to note when filling out tables.

✔ Place the cursor in the first cell of the table and type **1**, but do **NOT** press the *Enter* key.

Pressing the enter key will add another paragraph to a cell. It is not wrong to have multiple paragraphs in a table cell, but most of the time cells hold a single paragraph.

✔ Press the **TAB** key to move to the next cell in the table.

> **NOTE**: If you press the **TAB** key with the text cursor in the very last table cell, the system will automatically add a new row of cells to the table. You can also use the cursor control arrow keys to move between cells in a table.

When the text cursor is in a table cell, the **Table Tools** toolbar will open along the bottom of the display. This toolbar provides access to Table modification and formatting tools.

   ✔ Fill your table with information similar to that shown in Figure 6-2. (Remember to press the **TAB key** after each cell entry.)

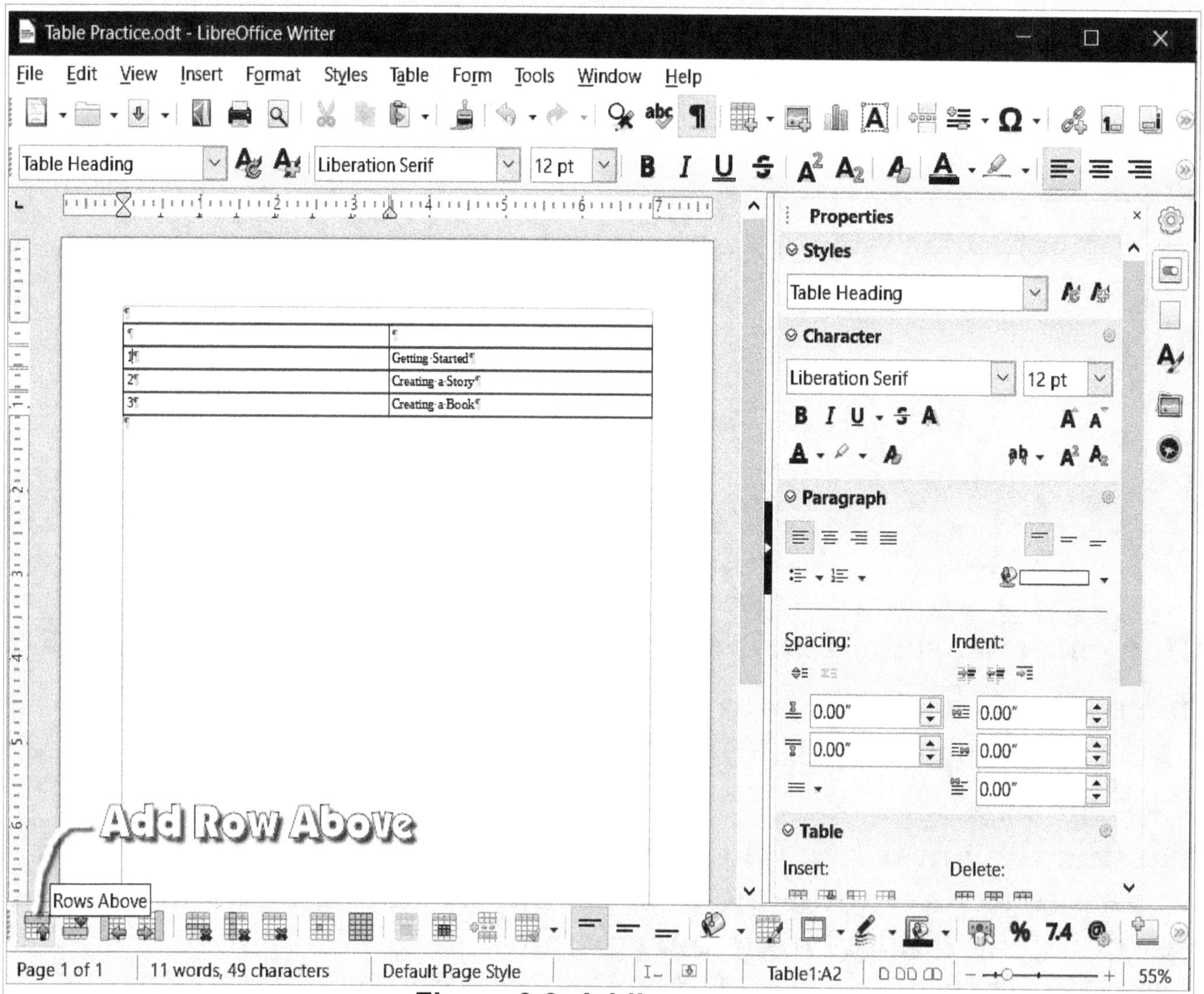

Figure 6-3, Adding a row.

   ✔ Place the text cursor in the **upper left** cell.

   ✔ Select the **Rows Above** tool from the Table toolbar.

This will add a new row above the cell where the text cursor is located. If you look at the Table *Toolbar* you will find tools for adding or deleting rows and columns.

- ✓ In the new upper left cell, enter **Project Number**.
- ✓ In the upper right cell, enter **Project Name**.
- ✓ Select the two top row cells and change the *Font* to **Bold, 14 pt** and the *Alignment* to **Center**.

Paragraphs in table cells have a *default* paragraph style. You can, of course, create your own special paragraph styles for table contents.

If you enter more text then will fit on one line, the system automatically uses *word wrap* to increase the row height as needed. In the example, the first column is much wider than required. There is an easy way to adjust table column widths.

- ✓ Move the cursor over the vertical line between Project Number and Project Name in the table and watch the cursor change to a double arrow.
- ✓ When the cursor changes to a *double arrow*, drag the vertical line to change the column width.

- ✓ To get complete control of table characteristics, first position the cursor somewhere in the table, and then from the *Menubar* select **Table, Properties.**

This will open the *Table Properties* dialog box that provides control over all table parameters (See Figure 6-4).

- ✓ Use the *Table Properties* dialog box to change the *Alignment* option to **Center**, and then enter a *Width* of **5.0**.

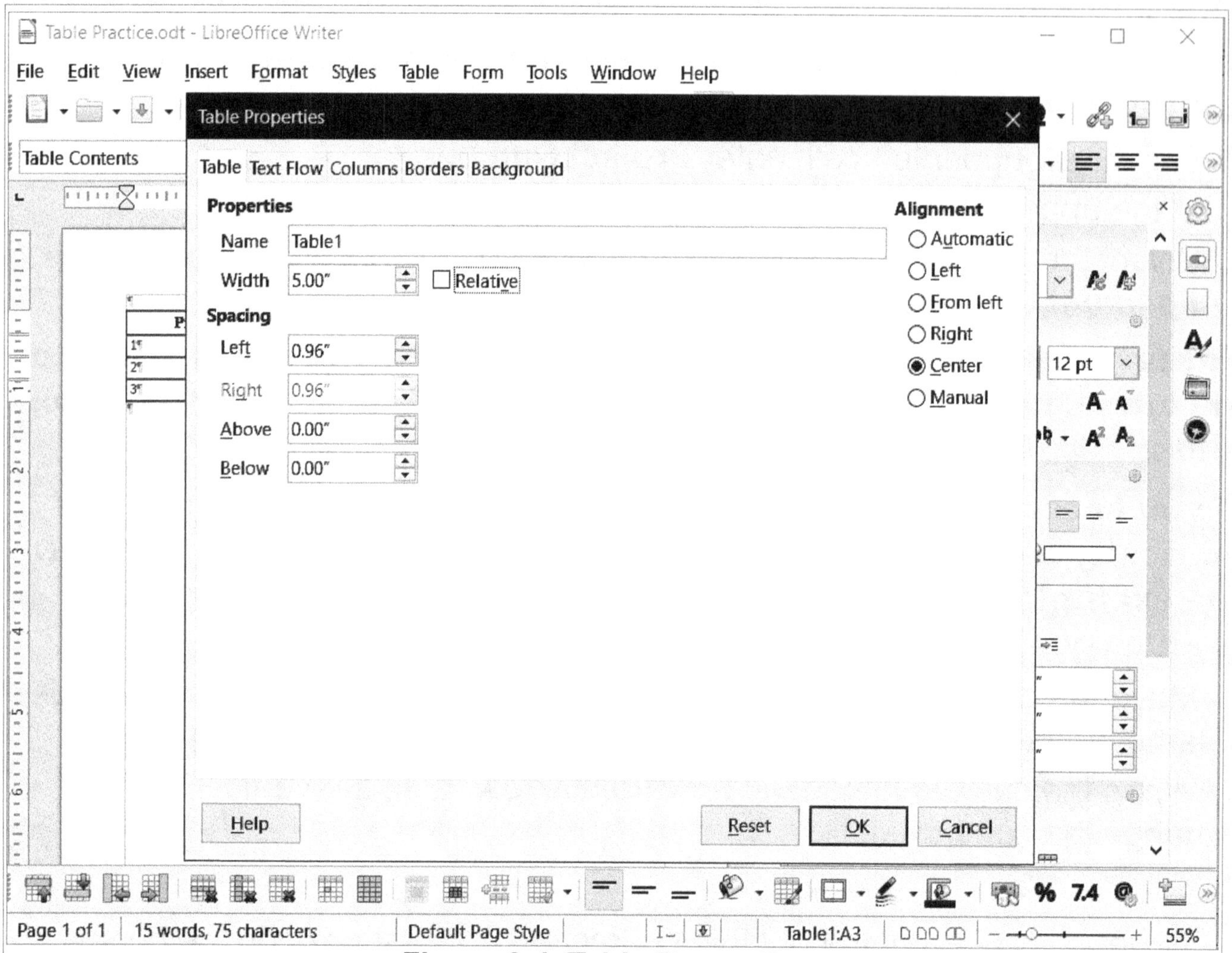

Figure 6-4, Table Properties.

✔ In the ***Table Properties*** dialog box, select the ***Columns TAB*** and set the ***Column Width*** for column 1 to **1.0**.

✔ In the ***Table Properties*** dialog box, select the ***Background TAB*** and set the ***Table*** (not Cell) ***Color*** to Pale **Yellow**.

✔ Select **OK** to close the ***Table Properties*** dialog box.

There are default paragraph styles for table cell text. You can use the method discussed in an earlier project to create custom paragraph styles for your tables. You can also modify the default style.

Placing the text cursor in a table cell will show the paragraph style for that cell. If you want to change the paragraph style for this cell, you can either create a custom paragraph style, or modify the default style.

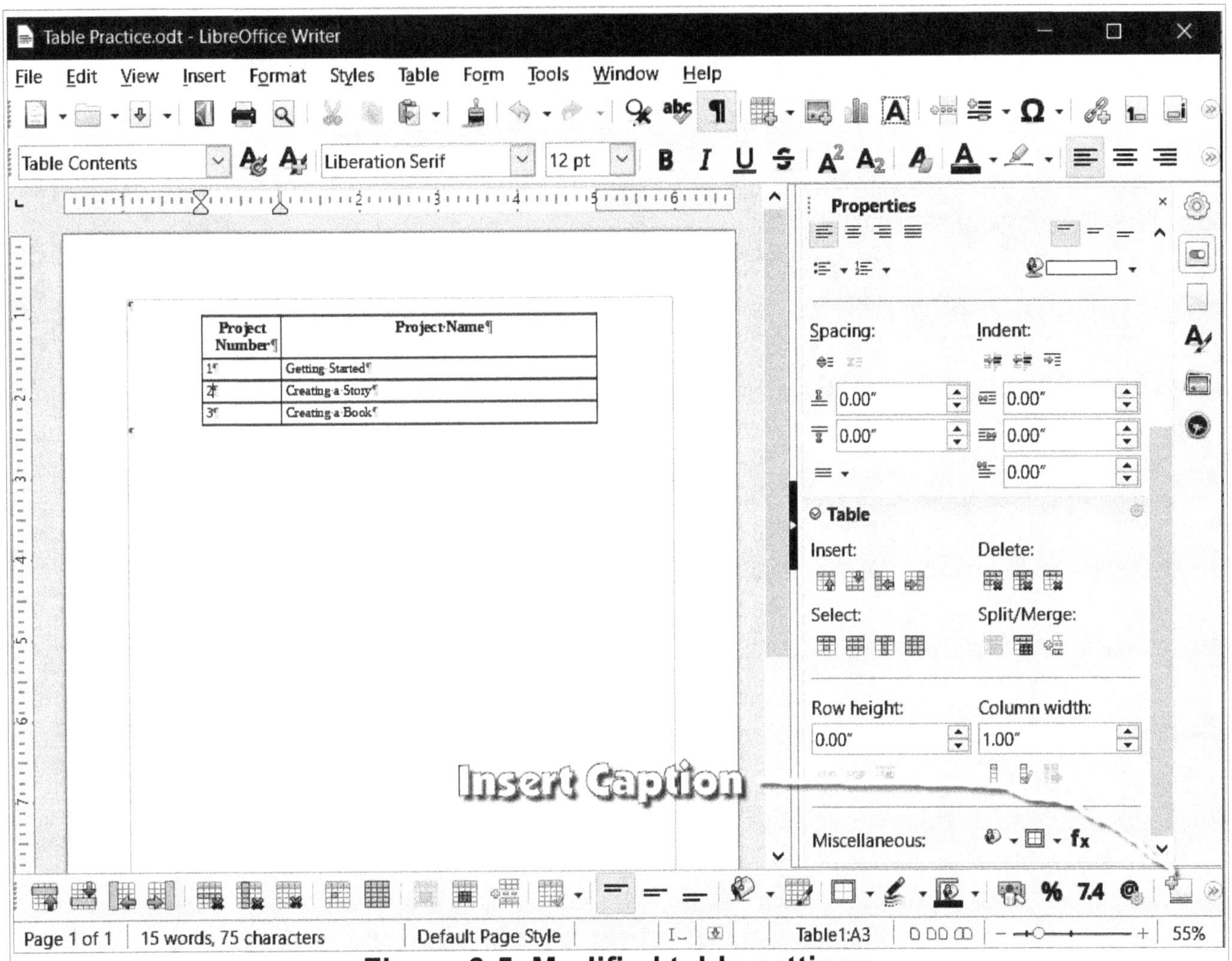

Figure 6-5, Modified table settings.

Another Table option is *Insert Caption*. Unlike captions for Images, this caption will appear above the table.

✔ Select the **Insert Caption** tool from the Table toolbar (see Figure 6-5).

✔ Note the **Category** option list in the **Insert Caption** dialog box.

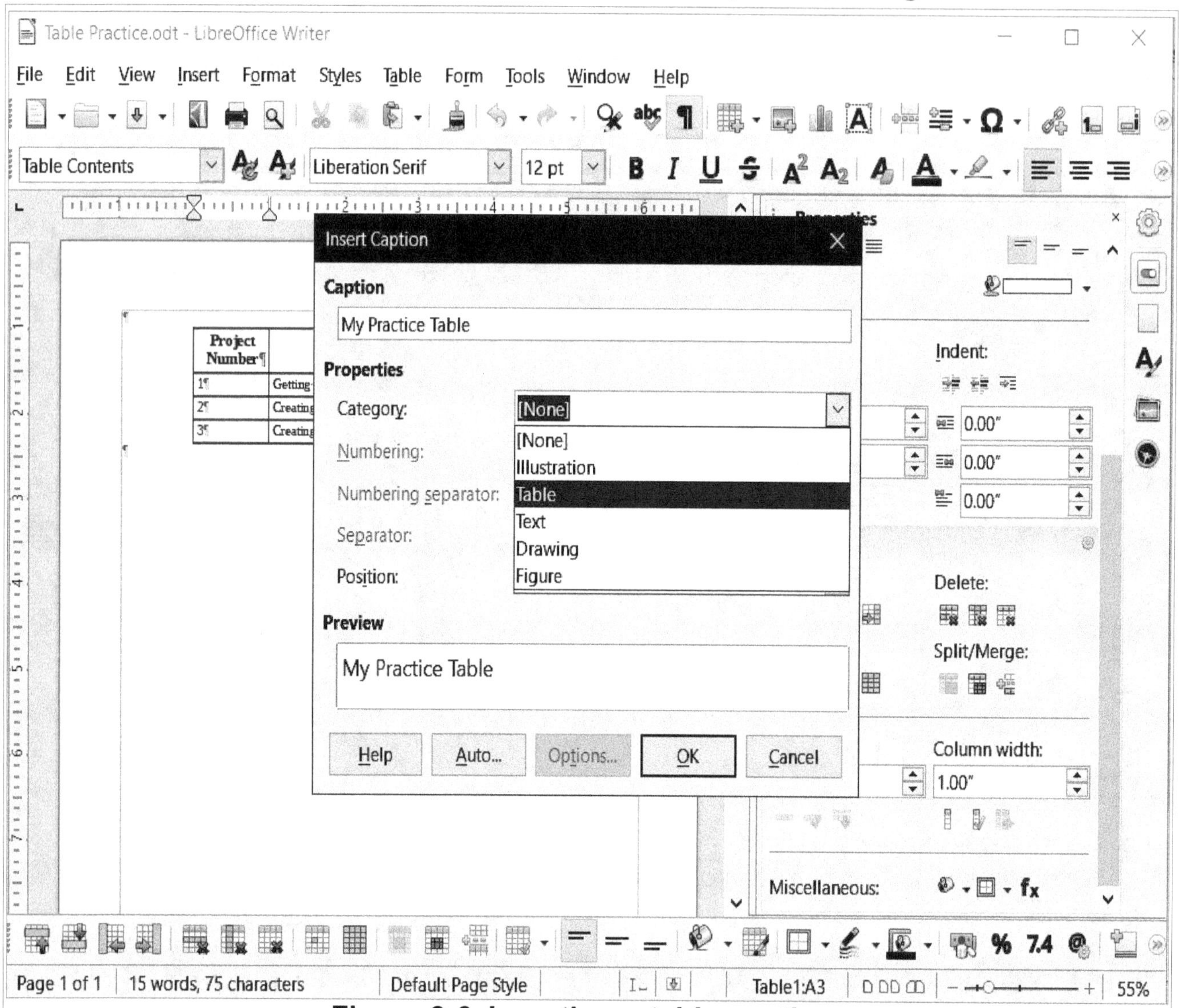

Figure 6-6, Inserting a table caption.

Note that there is a **Preview** box in the **Insert Caption** dialog box that shows what your caption will look like.

✔ Enter a caption for your table.

Captions can be edited after they are created.

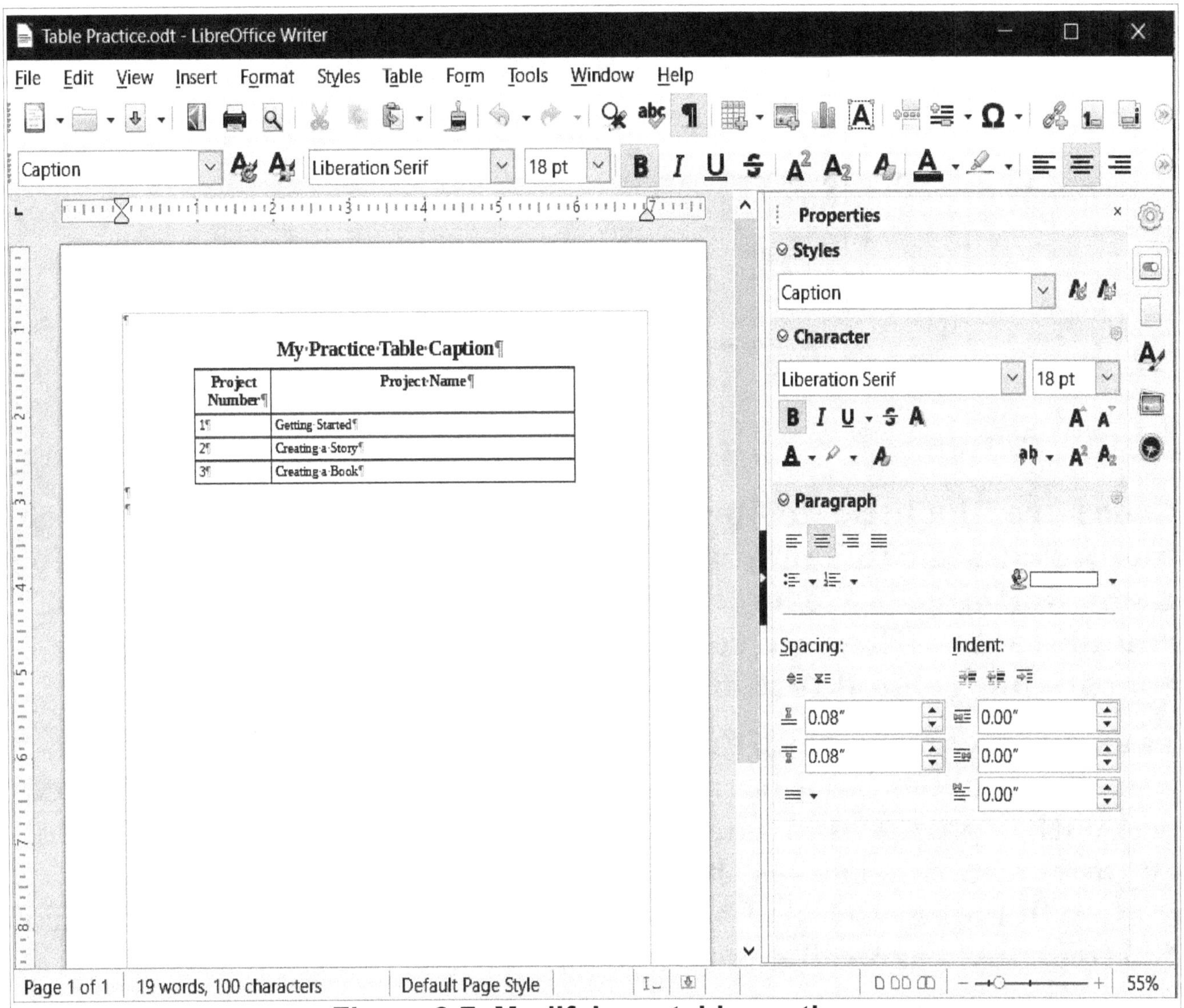

Figure 6-7, Modifying a table caption.

Tables can enhance your documents and take the pain out of aligning rows and columns. Tables in LibreOffice Writer can also include many functions found in spreadsheet software.

The example in Figure 6-8 was created directly in this LibreOffice Writer document. It uses date and currency formats (accessed through *Table, Number Format* from the *Menubar*), and also uses formulas to calculate totals and the sum of the last column. Good bye calculator!

Figure 6-8, Sample table with calculations.

Item	Purchase Date	Cost per Item	Qty	Total Cost
Book	December 5, 2017	$21.50	2	$43.00
Paper	November 3, 2017	$6.95	6	$41.70
Binders	November 3, 2017	$2.95	3	$8.85
Total				$93.55

Using Frames

Frames are like little documents that are inserted into a main document. Frames can contain the same kinds of things the main document contains, however, the main document body text flows around frames. They are sometimes used as sidebars to provide separate but related text or illustrations.

Frames can contain text, graphic images, or tables. Frames are typically *Anchored* to a paragraph in the main document. They can float with a paragraph. That means that if the text before a frame is edited, and this causes the paragraph to move, the anchored frame will move with it. The Wrap function can be used to control how text flows around a frame.

✓ Enter the following paragraphs after the table.

Frames added to list of useful tools.

Frames are like little documents that are inserted into a main document. They can contain the same things the main document contains. They are sometimes used as side-bars to provide separate but related text.

Frames can also contain graphics images or tables. Frames are typically anchored to a paragraph in the main document. They float with the paragraph. That means that if the text before a frame is edited, and this causes the anchor paragraph to move, the frame will move with it. The wrap function can be used to make text flow around a frame.

- ✓ Place the text cursor in the *Frames added to list of useful tools* paragraph, then set the *Paragraph Style* to **Heading 1**.

Next, a frame will be added to the document.

- ✓ Place the text cursor in the *Frames added to list of useful tools* paragraph, then from the *Menubar*, select **Insert, Frame, Frame**.

This opens the *Frame* dialog box. The *Type* tab of the dialog box provides for setting the width, height, and position of the frame.

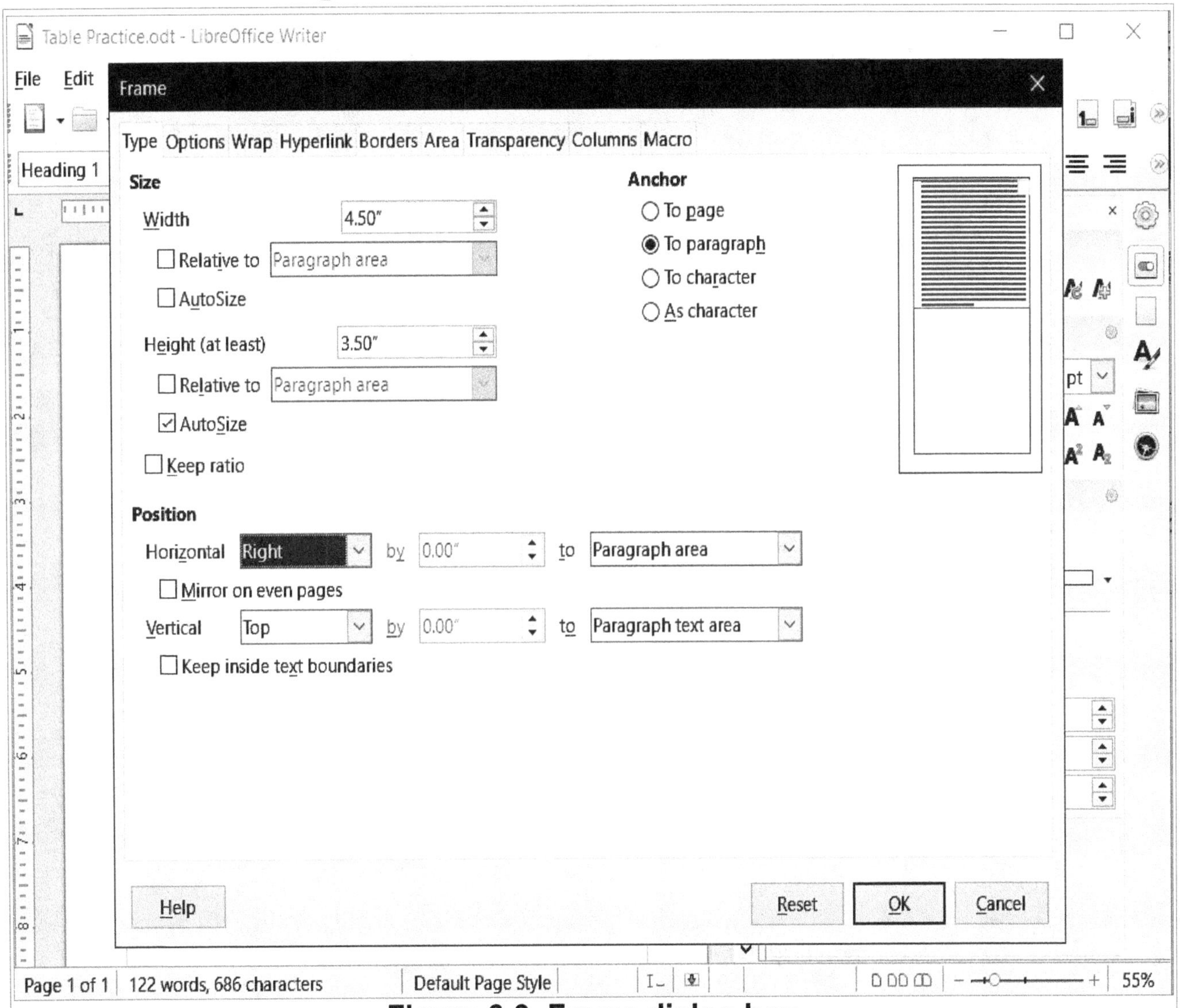

Figure 6-9, Frame dialog box.

- ✓ In the *Frame-Type* dialog box, set the *Width* to **4.50** and the *Height* to **3.5**.
- ✓ Set *Position, Horizontal* **Right**.
- ✓ Select *Anchor* to **Paragraph**.
- ✓ Select the *Wrap* tab and set *Wrap* to **Before**.

✔ Set **Borders** **ON**, then select **OK**.

✔ Place the text cursor in the frame and add some text. You should also experiment with inserting graphic images.

Tables and **Frames** provide ways to take your documents from the old typewriter page styles, to new professional style documents.

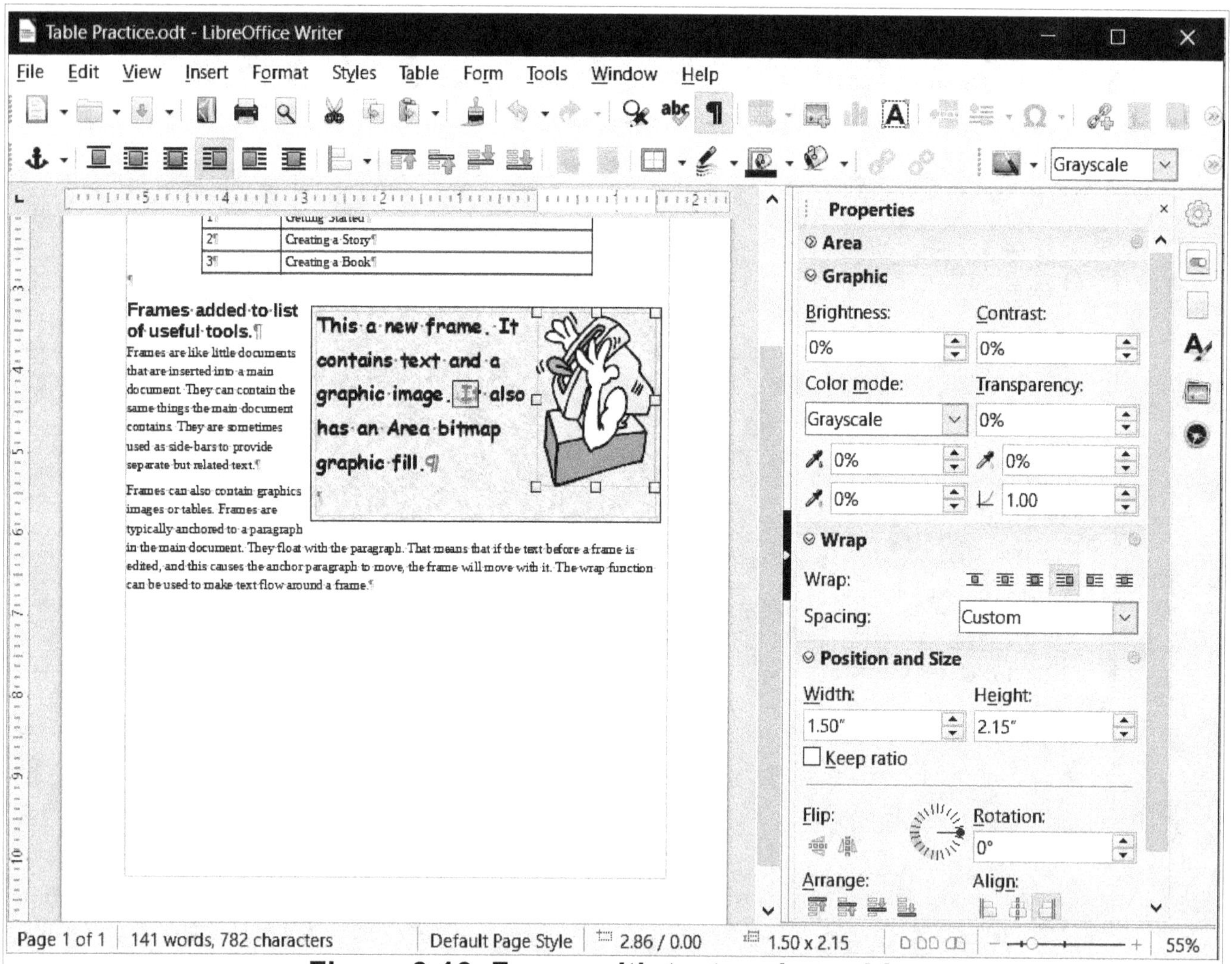

Figure 6-10, Frame with text and graphic.

LibreOffice Background

LibreOffice is is what is known as *Open Source* software. This means that the core code is in the public domain and can be downloaded and installed *for free.* The program has it's origin in StarOffice which was followed by OpenOffice. These programs were supported by Sun Micro Systems. After Sun Micro systems was acquired by Oracle, a number of the programmers were unhappy and split away to form the Document Foundation.

The Document Foundation (TDF) is a non-profit organization that promotes open-source document handling software. It was created by members of the OpenOffice.org community to manage and develop LibreOffice, a free and open-source office suite, and is legally registered in Germany as a Stiftung. Its goal is to produce a vendor-independent office suite with ODF support in a development environment free from corporate control.

The bottom line is that *The Document Foundation* consists of a large group of programmers who are continually upgrading the program features and making the program available for free, however, they do encourage donations to help support their efforts.

Downloading LibreOffice (Windows)

The first step is to use your web browser to locate the Document Foundation web site. The illustrations shown are from the *Firefox* web browser.

✓ Open your web browser and enter https://www.libreoffice.org/ in the address bar.

✓ Select **Download**.

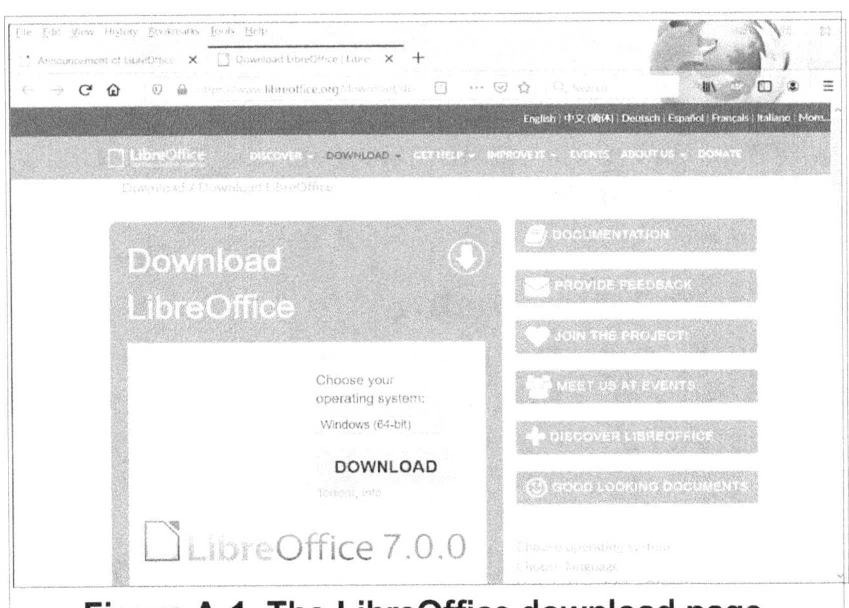

Figure A-1, The LibreOffice download page.

I have my *Firefox* ask me if I want to save the file, and this provides an opportunity to control where the download file is saved.

Figure A-2 shows that there is a built-in help program also available.

✔ Download the Built-in help program.

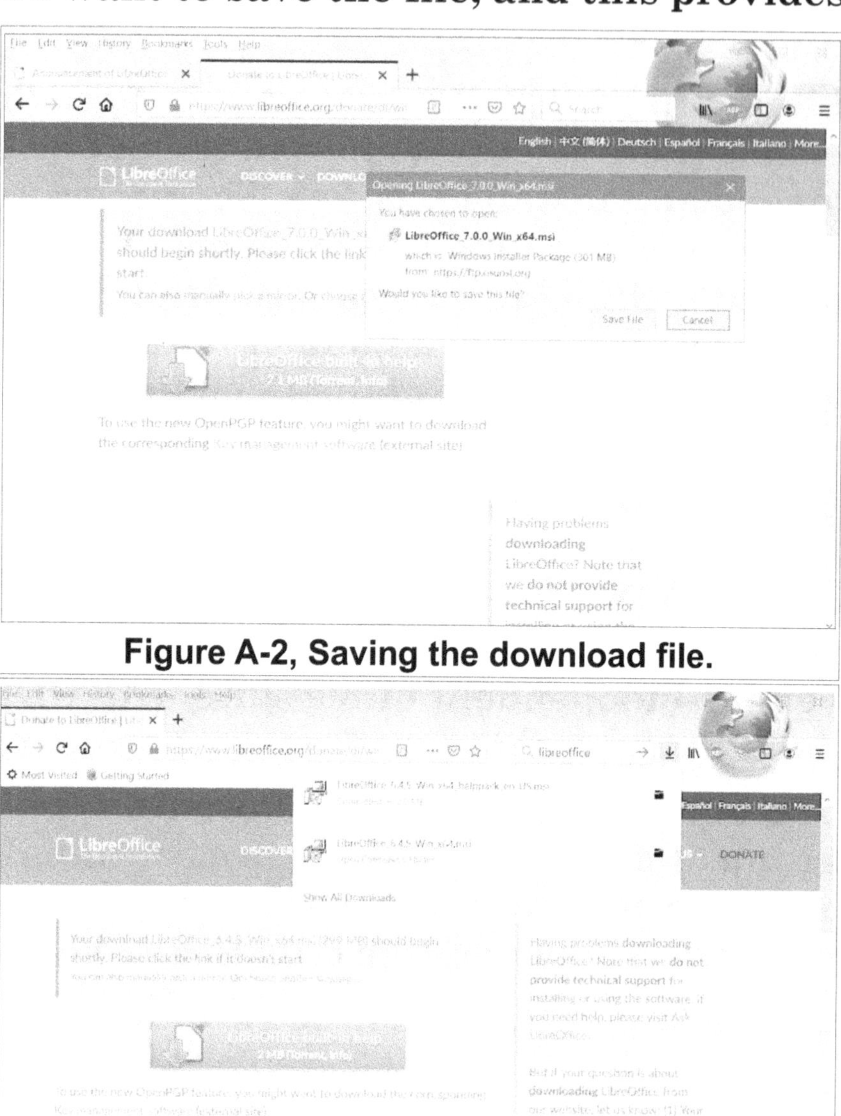

Figure A-2, Saving the download file.

In *Firefox*, there is a small arrow on the same line as the address bar. Selecting this arrow shows the progress of downloads. Figure A-3 shows Firefox has completed downloading the installation files.

✔ Once the downloads are complete, select each of them to begin the installation.

Figure A-3, Download progress.

The installation dialog box will show progress and will also prompt you to select various options. You should accept the default options.

✔ Install both **LibreOffice** and the **LibreOffice Help** files.

After the installations are complete, you have options (In Windows) to place a short-cut on the *Desktop*, on the *Taskbar*, or in the *Start* menu.

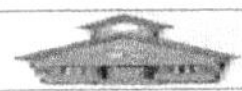

You should install the frequent updates as they appear. The good news is that updates will preserve your current documents and also the recent documents list.

Downloading LibreOffice (Linux)

Good News! Most versions of Linux automatically include LibreOffice. I currently prefer *Linux Mint.* The user interface for Linux Mint is very similar to Windows. If you have Linux Mint, you already have LibreOffice and Firefox.

BTW, Linux can be installed *for free* on older PCs that have Windows XP, Vista, or 7. Don't throw away an old Windows computer. It can live on with a Linux installation. 

Downloading LibreOffice (Mac)

Since I have avoided spending two or three times more than necessary for an overpriced Mac, I do not have screen shots. However if you Google, or Safari, *LibreOffice for mac*, you will find instructions and videos for Mac installation of LibreOffice.

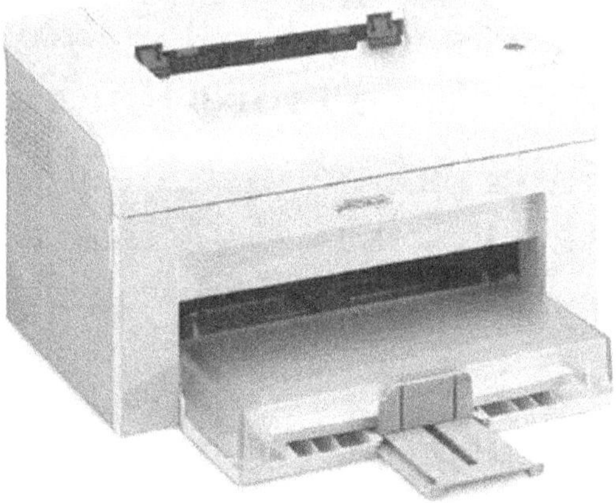

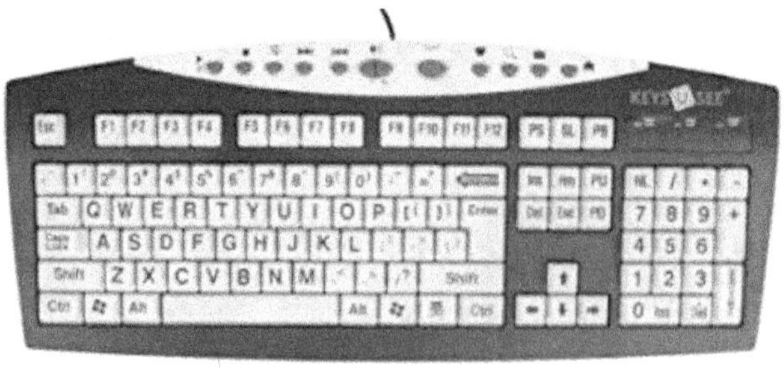

Appendix B ~ Computer Recommendations

Computer Hardware

If you are serious about doing word processing, you need a serious computer. Small netbook or laptop computers can cause frustration because of strange keyboards, or inadequate resolution, screen size, and storage. Some folks like the idea of portability, but serious writers establish a comfortable work place with room to spread out the related research papers and pictures needed for their projects.

Prices for desktop computers, either with a tower case or pizza box style case are relatively low. At the time of this writing, new desktop computers adequate for desktop publishing can be found for less than $600. From time to time refurbish computer suppliers acquire large volumes from company upgrading or downsizing, clean them up, and sell them for below $200. There are great bargains for good shoppers. Walmart, Amazon, and Big Box stores like the Micro Center will occasionally have refurbished bargains.

I do not recommend 'all-in-one' computers. They tend to be over-priced and are nearly impossible to fix when they go bad... and they will. Also, computers advertised for seniors are to be avoided. They are always overpriced, not really much easier than regular PC's, and are not very flexible. This opinion is based on over 10 years providing tech support to the Bristol Village retirement community Computer Club where our senior residents have almost every type of computer and every possible problem.

For Windows 10, look for at least 8GB of RAM. Unless you will also be doing video editing or playing 3D graphics games, most any current desktop computer out there will be adequate for desktop publishing. For desktop publishing and basic Internet searching, $1,000 is too much to pay for a new computer.

If you have an old outdated Windows PC with at least 4GB of RAM and a decent size 1920 by 1080 monitor, don't throw it out. You can

install *Linux Mint*, it will look a lot like your old PC, and it comes with *LibreOffice, Firefox*, and *Thunderbird* (for email). The good news is that Linux is *free.*

Sorry Mac cult members, Mac hardware is always 2 to 3 times more expensive than equivalent PC hardware. Unless your eyes are way above average, or you want to wear magnifying specs all day, avoid those 13 or 15 inch displays.

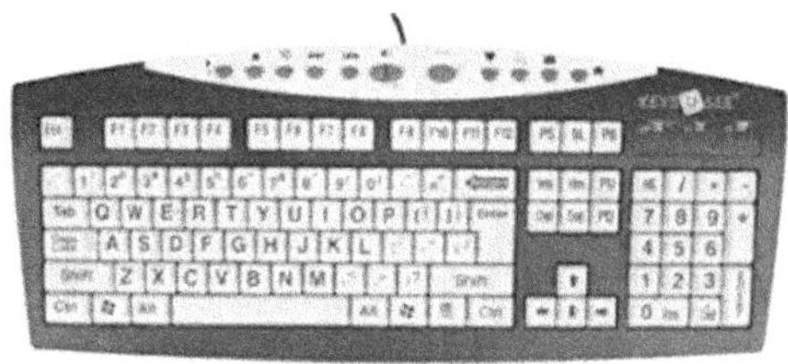

I recommend a 22 or 24 inch flat screen monitor with at least 1920 by 1080 resolution. You can find 24 inch monitors for a little over $100, and 22 inch monitors for under $100. Larger screen size can give you tennis neck. Dual monitors, however, can be very useful. You can keep your document open on one monitor and use the other for Internet searching or manipulating graphics.

You will also need a decent keyboard. I like the *Keys-U-See Large Print* US English USB Wired Yellow Keyboard, Standard Size Keys with Large Letters. Some folks prefer a backlight keyboard for better low light visibility.

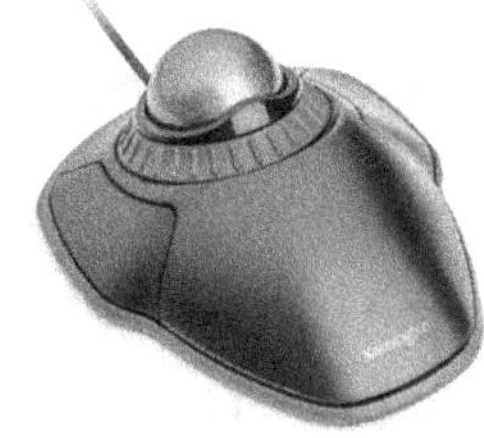

You will also need a mouse. Try to find one that fits your hand. If you are experiencing loss of finger dexterity, consider a track ball alternative to the mouse. An advantage of track balls is that they stay in one place as opposed to the mouse which has to be moved around the desk.

Printers

Printers are available as either ink jet or laser. Ink jet printers are cheap, but ink cartridges are not. Also, ink can dry up and is not good for occasional users. Laser printers use dry powder and are typically more reliable. Multi-function, or all-in-one printers can be used as copy machines or to scan documents. However, if all you want to do is print documents in black and white, consider a monochrome laser printer. You can find a decent monochrome laser printer that will print on both sides for around $100. Color laser printers start around $300.

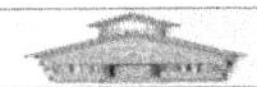

External Hard Drives and Flash Drives

An external hard drive is a must for backing up files and moving files from one computer to another. You can get more USB 3 storage for under $100 then you will ever need for even the largest book files you are likely to create. They are also very good places to archive files from your digital cameras.

The price of flash drives keep coming down. Less then $10 can get you a flash drive with up to 128 GB of storage space. They are easy to use (and small so they are also easy to lose), and easy to move files from one computer to another. Because the mean time between failure of flash drives is not as good as hard drives, I don't recommend them as an alternative for active storage of documents files.

.doc .jpg
.png

Appendix C ~ Organizing Files

Introduction

If you are new to computing, you may be frustrated when you try to find document or picture files. If you simply *Save* a file, it may or may not end up in a place where you can find it again. LibreOffice remembers the last place files were saved, and this might not be the place where you want your new files to end up. After you have been working on a number of different documents, you will want to back up your files... somewhere. This document will show how to manage your files using *File Explorer* in Windows 10.

Opening a File Explorer Window

✔ To open a *File Explorer Window*, hold the **Windows Key** down and press the **E** key.

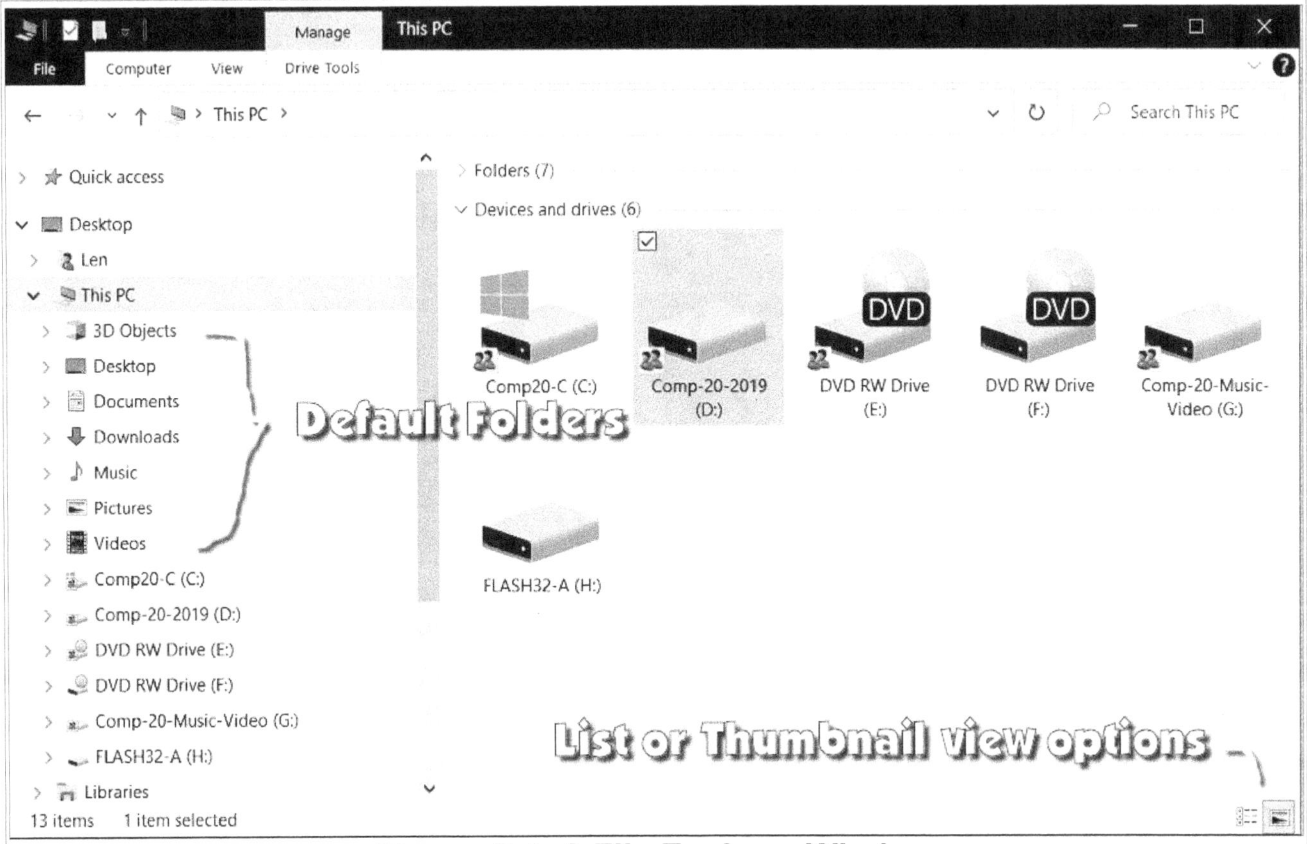

Figure C-1, A File Explorer Window.

Figure C-1 shows a *File Explorer Window* with the **This PC** option selected. The Thumbnail view option has been turned **ON**.

The figure shows that the computer has 2 DVD Drives installed (E: and F:), 3 hard drives installed (C:, D:, and G:), and a flash drive (H:) installed. Every PC will have a C: drive. The other drives are optional and the drive letters are assigned by the system.

The column on the left side of the display in Figure C-1 shows a list of the installed drives. Above the C: drive there is a list of default folders. Unless you take control by using *File, Save As*, application programs (apps) will use a default folder.

✔ Select the **C:** drive in the *File Explorer* window.

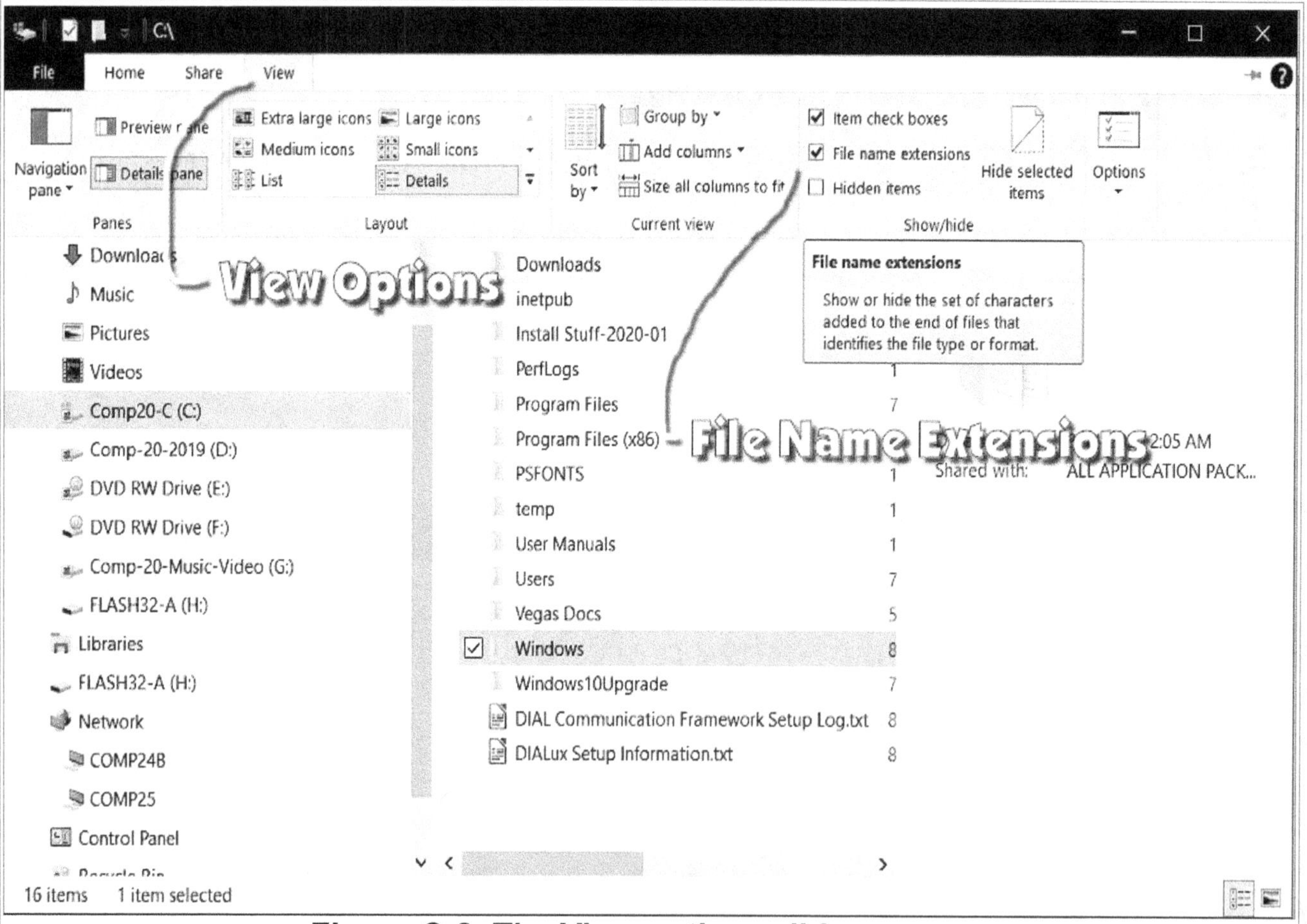

Figure C-2, The View options ribbon menu.

✔ Select the **View** tab in the *File Explorer* window.

The *View* ribbon menu provides a number of viewing options. The options are grouped from left to right; *Panes, Layout, Current view*, and *Show/hide*.

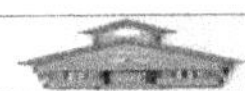

✓ Make sure that the **Item check boxes** and **File name extensions** are checked.

> 
>
> Data is organized differently in text documents than it is in picture or graphics files. To tell one type of file format from another, a three letter *file name extension* is added to the end of the file name. For example, if you save a document using **LibreOffice Writer** and name the document with the name *MyFile*, the name of the file that is saved will be **MyFile.odt**. If you save a similar document using Microsoft Word, it will be **MyFile.doc.** If you create a picture using a paint program and name it *MyFile*, the file that is saved might be *MyFile.jpg* or *MyFile.png*. (There are several different formats for picture or image files including *jpg* and *png*.)

When you want to retrieve your document or picture, the system can tell from the three letter file name extension the difference between document and picture files, and knows which program to use to open the file. When you are using *File Explorer*, it is important for you to know what format each file uses. This is why you should have the **File name extensions** option turned **ON**.

In Figure C-3, observe that in the list on the left side of the window that there are either **>** arrows, or **v** arrows, or nothing to the left of the entries. Selecting a **v** arrow will list the contents of that folder. Selecting a **>** arrow will show a list of files in that folder.

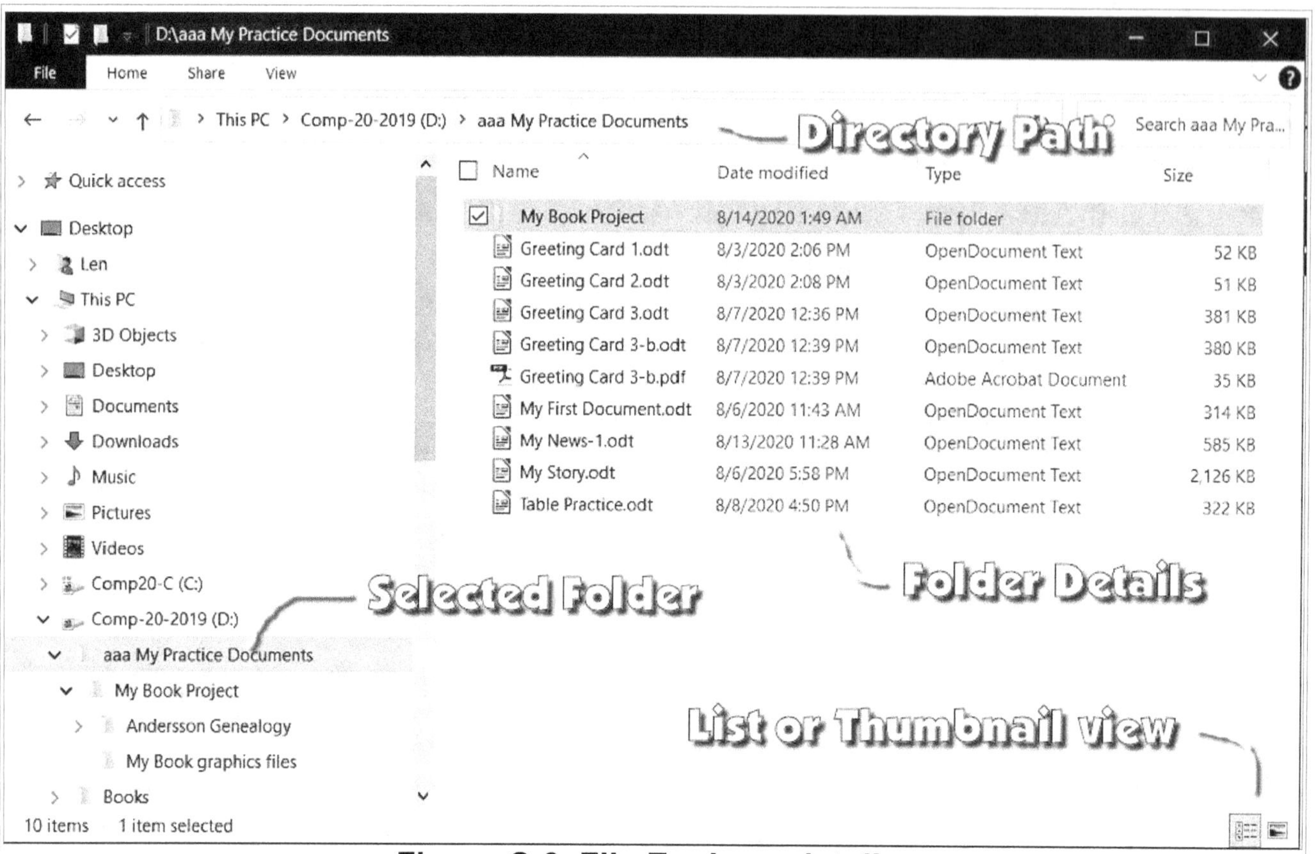

Figure C-3, File Explorer details.

The ***directory path*** (see Figure C-3) shows the location of the currently selected folder. Figure C-3 shows that the ***aaa My Practice Documents*** folder has been selected, and it lives in the ***Comp-20-2019 (D:)*** hard drive in ***This PC***. Since there can be folders inside of folders inside of folders in different drives, it is important to use the directory path reminder to see where you are.

The drive list on the left side of ***Figure C-3*** shows that the ***aaa My Practice Documents*** folder in the ***Comp-20-2019 (D:)*** drive is selected. The list of files in this folder is displayed using the ribbon tools ***View, Details*** option. The ***Details*** list shows the ***Name, Date Modified, Type***, and ***Size*** of each file in the folder.

> **NOTE:** When the ***Details*** view option is used, you can sort the list simply by selecting a column heading. Each time you select a column heading the list will switch between ***ascending*** and ***descending***.

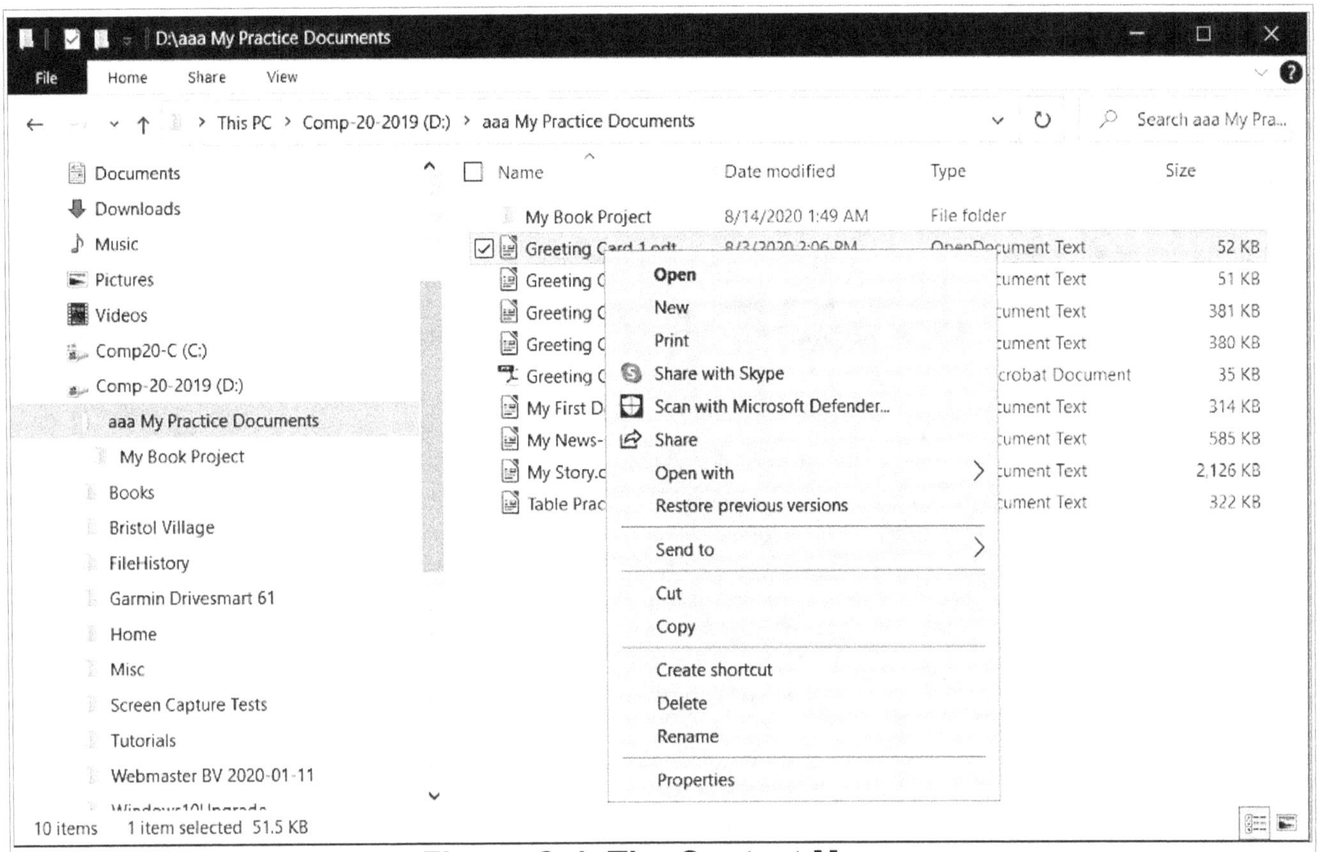

The following is a screenshot of a File Explorer window showing a context menu:

Name	Date modified	Type	Size
My Book Project	8/14/2020 1:49 AM	File folder	
Greeting Card 1.odt	8/3/2020 2:06 PM	OpenDocument Text	52 KB
Greeting C...		...ument Text	51 KB
Greeting C...		...ument Text	381 KB
Greeting C...		...ument Text	380 KB
Greeting C...		...crobat Document	35 KB
My First D...		...ument Text	314 KB
My News-...		...ument Text	585 KB
My Story.c...		...ument Text	2,126 KB
Table Prac...		...ument Text	322 KB

Context Menu options: Open, New, Print, Share with Skype, Scan with Microsoft Defender…, Share, Open with, Restore previous versions, Send to, Cut, Copy, Create shortcut, Delete, Rename, Properties.

Figure C-4, The Context Menu.

If you *right click* on a file or folder in the *Details* list, a *Context Menu* will appear (see Figure C-4). Make a note of the options available in the *Context Menu*.

You should have a *File Explorer* window open on your computer.

✔ Try selecting the arrows beside the different entries and observe the effect on the display.

✔ Locate your Practice folder created while completing the Projects in this book.

✔ Display the *Details* view for your Practice folder.

✔ Right click on a folder or file name and observe the *Context Menu* options.

NOTE: One of the file *Access Options* in Windows 10 is *One Drive*. This is a collection of hard drives in the '*cloud*' that are owned and controlled by Microsoft, and require an Internet connection and an active Microsoft Account to use. Because I am a control freak and want to own and control my files, I *never* use cloud storage. There may be some advantage for some people who do not want to maintain their own hard drives, or who need access to files from different computers in different locations. But, I prefer to have complete control of my files. Companies that offer cloud storage are taking control and ownership of peoples personal files, in my opinion a bad idea for most users.

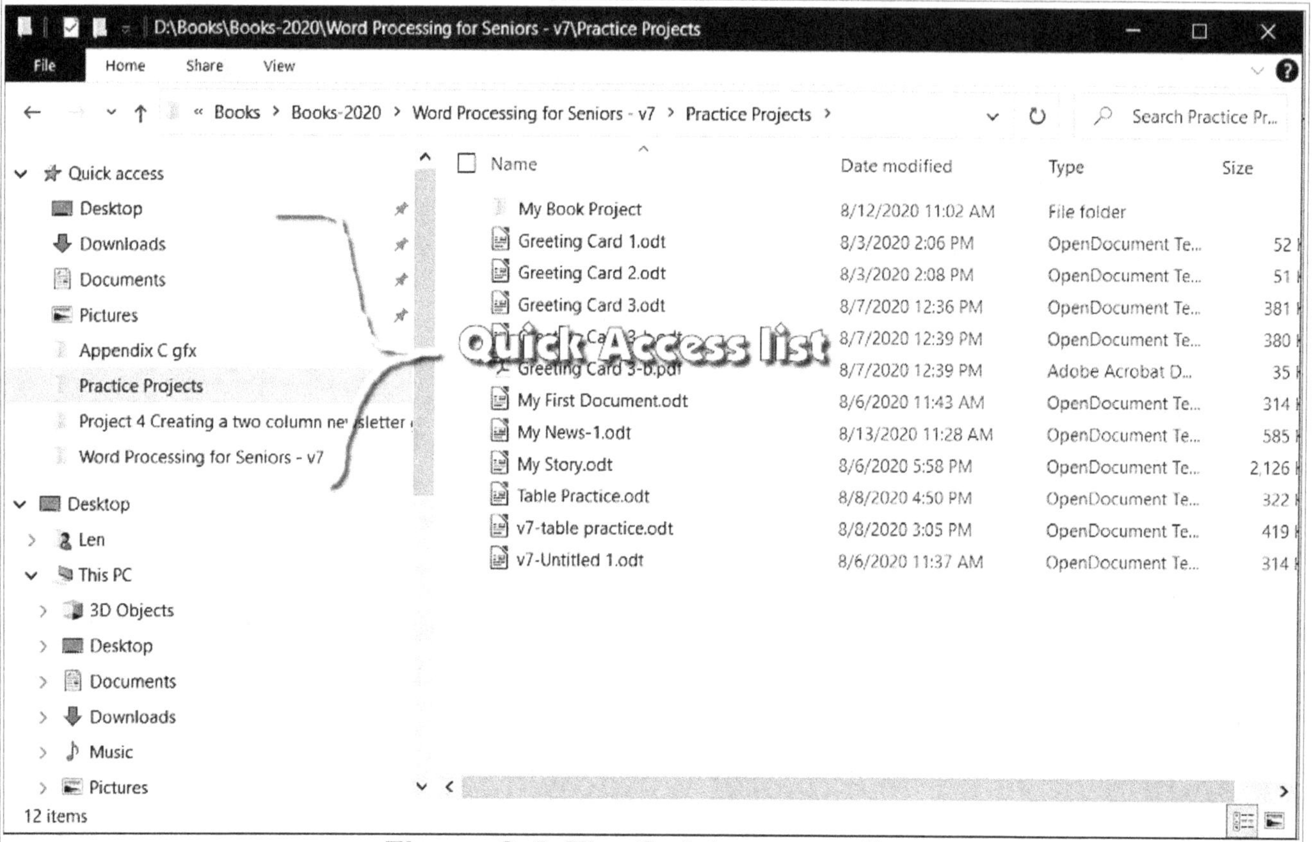

Figure C-5, The Quick access list.

The **Quick Access** option shows lists of recently accessed folders and data files. The **Quick Access** list can be opened or closed by selecting the small arrow to the left side of the **Quick Access** option.

The **This PC** option shows a list of the different drives installed on the computer. If you insert a flash drive or a camera memory card, the drive will appear on this list. In Figure C-6, a flash drive that has been renamed **FLASH32-A** is included in the list of drives.

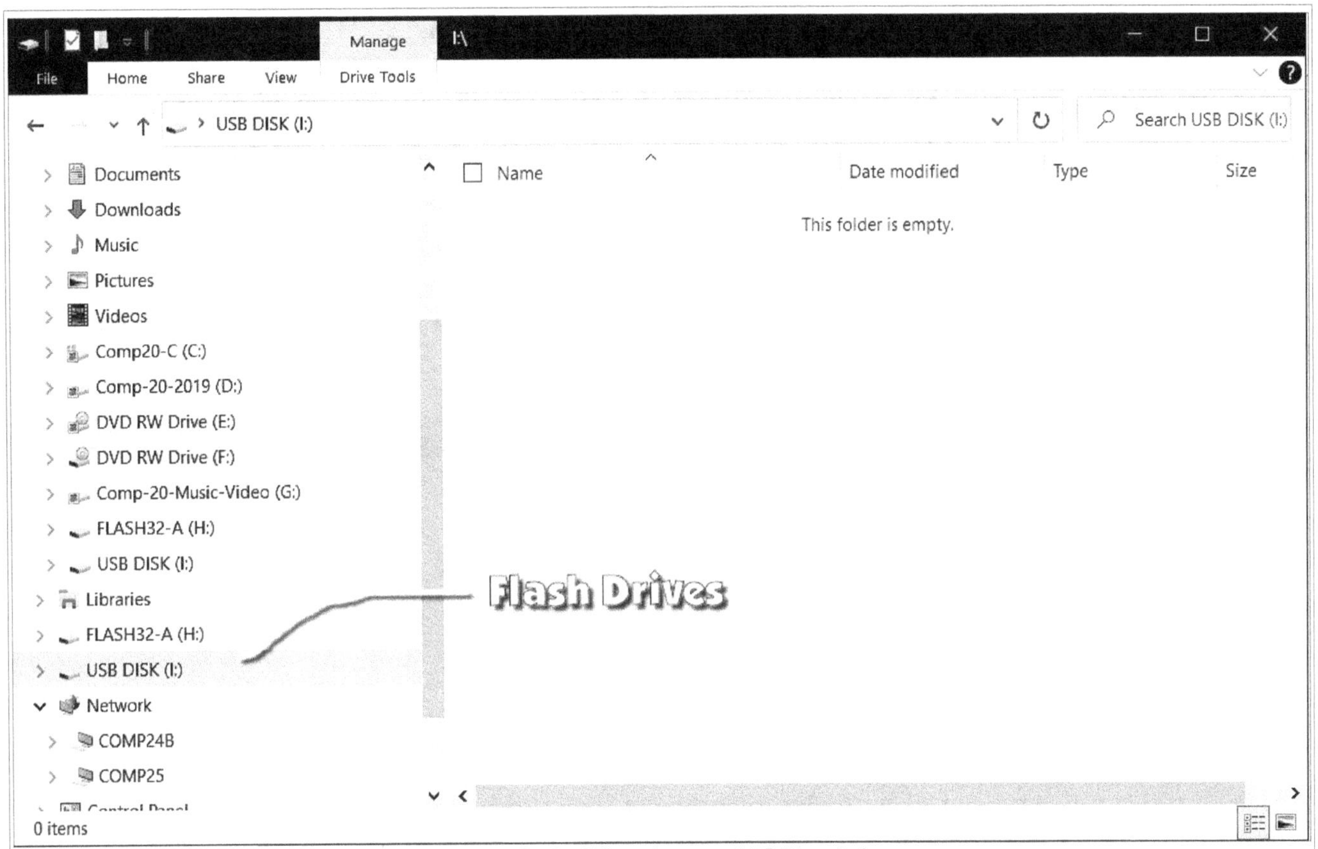

Figure C-6, Flash, or USB, drives.

You can rename flash drives. *Right click* on the drive in the list and select the **Rename** option from the *Context Menu*.

In Figure C-6, two USB flash drives have been installed. One has been renamed to **FLASH32-A**, while the other has the default name. I recommend that you rename your flash drives to remind yourself which is which. If you have a box full of flash drives it might be hard to remember what is on each drive. Because I have collected a lot of these flash drives, I tape a small label to each one.

> **NOTE**: *File Explorer* shows flash drives, external hard drives, and SD cards from cameras. You can use the same file management options on any of these different kinds of drives.

The *Network* option (see Figure C-6) shows a list of the different computers available if the computer is part of a local area network. The local network administrator must set permissions on these drives before they can be accessed from different network computers.

Copying Files From One Drive To Another

The *File Explorer* makes copying folders or files from drive to another very easy. Our old friends **Copy** and **Paste** do the job.

- ✔ To Copy a file (or folder) from one drive to another, **right click on** the file to copy and select **Copy** from the *Context Menu*.

- ✔ Select the ***destination drive*** (or destination folder), ***right click***, and select **Paste** from the *Context Menu*.

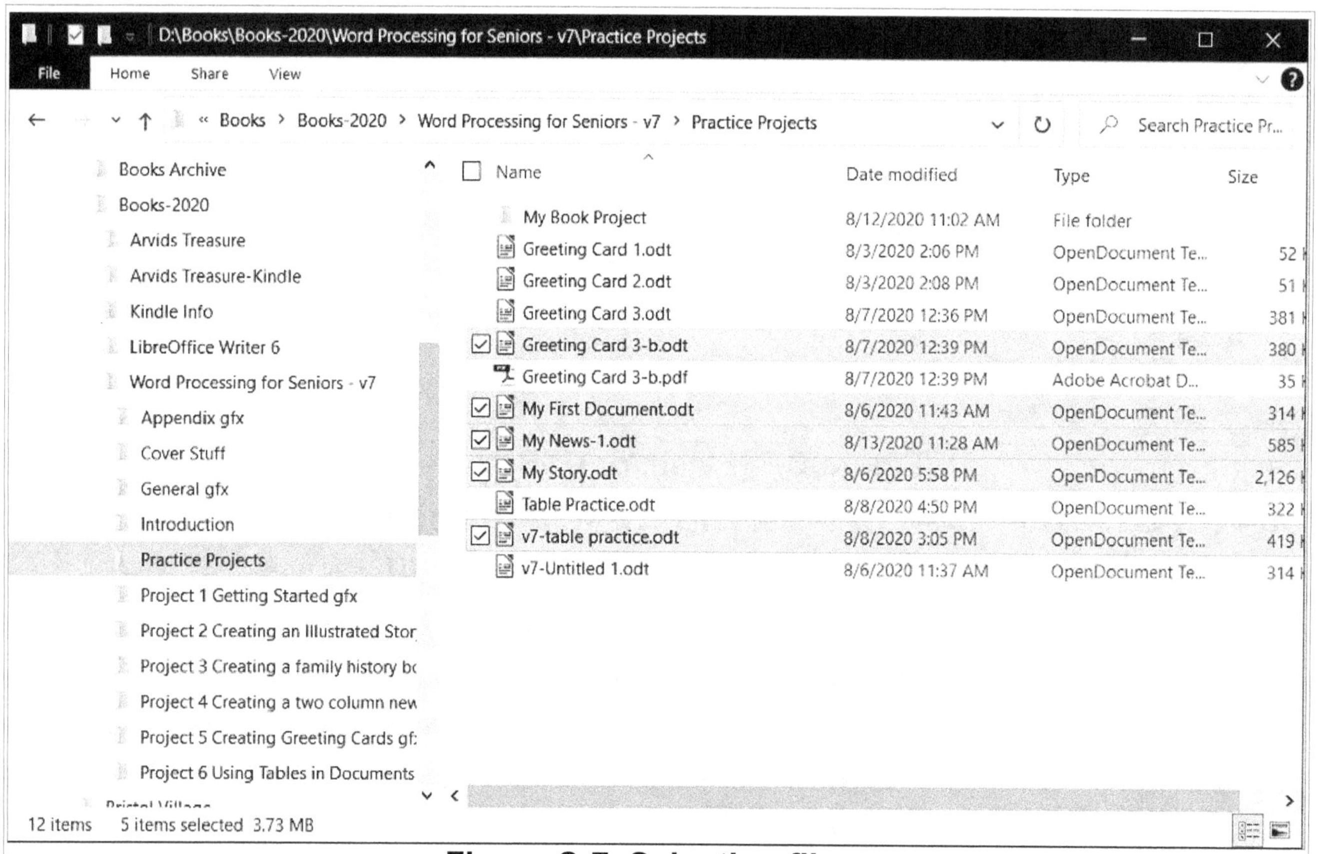

Figure C-7, Selecting files.

It is possible to select multiple files or folders to copy at the same time. If you followed the earlier step and toggled *View Check boxes ON*, you can use the check boxes to select multiple files.

You can also use **Ctrl+A** to select *all* files.

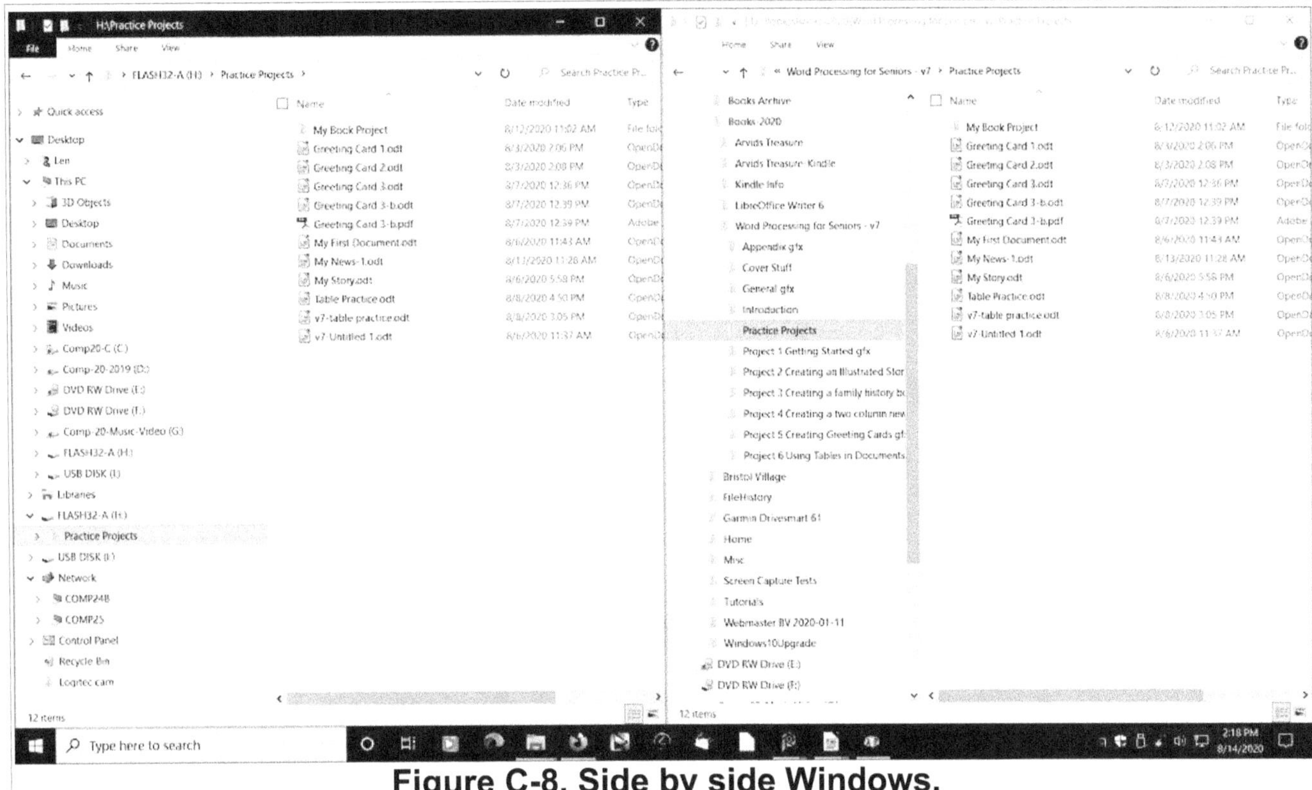

Figure C-8, Side by side Windows.

Let's say you are backing up files from one drive to another. There is a Windows trick that provides for having two Windows open side-by-side at the same time (see Figure C-8).

✓ Press **Windows Key+E** to open a *File Explorer* Window.

✓ Press **Windows Key+E** to open a second *File Explorer* Window.

✓ Select the *first* File Explorer Window and press **Windows Key + the *right* cursor control arrow key**.

✓ Select the *second* File Explorer Window and press **Windows Key + the *left* cursor control arrow key**.

With the two File Explorer Windows open side-by-side, it is easier to copy files from one place to another.

Flash drives are very handy for moving files from one place to another. However, I do not recommend them for permanent backup files. The mean time between failure of flash drives is not as good as traditional hard drives. The cost of high capacity exter-nal hard drives is so low these days, I recommend that you use an external hard drive for backing up important files. The paranoids

among us even keep their eternal hard drives in a separate location.

When your computer crashes or your hard drive dies, and it will, at the worst possible time, you will end up with a large blue bruise on your forehead if you do not have external backup of your important files.

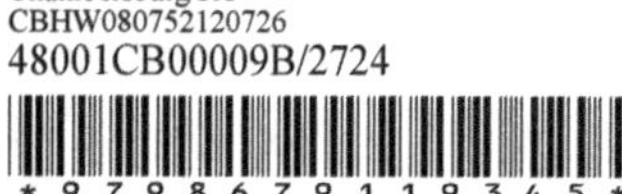